COMRADE
HUPPERT

COMRADE HUPPERT

A Poet in Stalin's World

GEORGE HUPPERT

INDIANA UNIVERSITY PRESS   *Bloomington & Indianapolis*

This book is a publication of

INDIANA UNIVERSITY PRESS
Office of Scholarly Publishing
Herman B Wells Library 350
1320 East 10th Street
Bloomington, Indiana 47405 USA

iupress.indiana.edu

The paper used in this publication
meets the minimum requirements of
the American National Standard for
Information Sciences—Permanence
of Paper for Printed Library
Materials, ANSI Z39.48–1992.

*Manufactured in the
United States of America*

*Library of Congress
Cataloging-in-Publication Data*

Names: Huppert, George, 1934– author
Title: Comrade Huppert : a poet in
  Stalin's world / George Huppert.
Description: Bloomington : Indiana
  University Press, 2016. | Includes
  bibliographical references and index.
  Identifiers: LCCN 2015030953| ISBN
  9780253019783 (cloth : alk. paper) |
  ISBN 9780253019844 (ebook)
Subjects: LCSH: Huppert, Hugo. |
  Authors, Austrian—20th century—
  Biography. | Translators—Austria—
  Biography.
Classification: LCC PT2617.U725 Z65
  2016 | DDC 838/.91409—dc23
LC record available at http://
  lccn.loc.gov/2015030953

1 2 3 4 5   21 20 19 18 17 16

*This book is dedicated to the memory of my parents,
Dr. Edmund and Irma Huppert. Together with their own parents,
their brothers and sisters, and virtually the entire Jewish communities
of Teschen and Bielitz, they were murdered in Auschwitz.*

CONTENTS

ACKNOWLEDGMENTS

The author thanks the archivists and librarians who made his research possible, especially Christina Moeller of the Akademie der Künste in Berlin and Dr. Deborah Rose-Lefmann of Northwestern University. Robert Sloan of the Indiana University Press has been an ideal editor, and Harriet Lightman remains the author's indispensable collaborator.

NOTE ON TRANSLATION

All translations are mine, unless otherwise noted. Cities in the multi-ethnic Austrian empire and its successors almost always had a German name as well as a second version, as in Lemberg/Lwów. Depending on the time and the circumstances, I have tried to use the German name or the Slavic one, following Hugo Huppert's usage, which usually favors the German name he grew up with, as in Teschen and Bielitz.

COMRADE
HUPPERT

INTRODUCTION

I NEVER KNEW HUGO HUPPERT. I WAS NOT AWARE OF HIS existence until years after his death. By chance, I found his three-volume autobiography on a shelf in the University of Cincinnati Library, which I happened to be visiting. Those books were rare items. Only one of his books was translated into English, and that was his *Men of Siberia* (1934). Originally published in Moscow that year, the book was made available to Communist sympathizers in New York and London, at a time when there was a good deal of sympathy for the Soviet Union in the West, just one year after Hitler's seizure of power and before the Moscow Trials revealed the brutal face of Stalin's world.

I started reading the first of the three autobiographical volumes and I was completely taken with the author's account of his growing up in Bielitz, on the eve of the First World War. Bielitz was part of the Austrian Empire, a largely German-speaking city surrounded by Polish-speaking villages. I hardly knew anything about Bielitz, but I was born in the city of Teschen, only a few miles away, another German-speaking island in a sea of Polish and Czech villages.

My interest in the author's account of his family's experiences might not have carried me much further had I not noted that Hugo was born only a few months after my own father's birth, in 1902. There were other similarities as well. Both boys left their hometowns to pursue advanced degrees, Hugo in political science, my father in chemistry. I was slightly intrigued—was the previously unknown Hugo Huppert a relative?— and found to my surprise that I could not bring myself to put the memoir

1

down: there was something familiar in Hugo's voice, in his language, his storytelling. It was just a completely absorbing book.

My next step was to order the three volumes from an antiquarian book dealer in Berlin. He was able to add some other titles, several books of Hugo's poetry, and his Italian travel book, *Münzen im Brunnen* (Coins in the Fountain), among others. This hardly exhausted the huge bibliography of Hugo Huppert's works. There are other volumes of poetry, the adaptations of Mayakovsky's poetry, and the adaptation of the Georgian national epic, Shota Rustaveli's *Vitiaz' v tigrovoi shkure* (*The Knight in the Tiger Skin*).

I started reading seriously now, especially the autobiographical books. Gradually I began to realize that it was not only the charm of Hugo's writing that had me spellbound: it was also the story of his life, a life that was an almost perfect embodiment of a twentieth-century experience—if you happened to be born in Europe, especially in eastern and central Europe, between 1900 and the 1950s, when the killings of two world wars were extended by the mass murder of innocent civilians on the orders of two half-mad backcountry politicians, Djugashvili (Stalin) and Schicklgruber (Hitler).

At this point in my reading, in my discovery of Hugo's writings, I decided to write a book about Hugo's life. Not a biography, exactly, but the story of a poet whose life is perfectly representative of those men, women, and children who had the misfortune of coming into the world at the wrong time and in the wrong place. Especially if they were Jewish, they were not likely to survive the events set in motion in the 1920s.

Before the wars, before the collapse of empires, growing up in a town like Bielitz would have been something close to an idyllic experience. Still, even here, in this prosperous place full of industry and surrounded by lush forests and mountain ranges, it was not possible to avoid entirely the first stirrings of the madness to come. In the first two chapters of this book, I draw a contrast between the apparently idyllic life of the boy Hugo, growing up in Bielitz, and the violence in Vienna and in the provinces.

Right up to his departure for Vienna, in 1920, Hugo had been exactly what you would expect from a well brought up son of middle-class parents in a provincial city. He wrote poetry, he had a serious interest in music, and he loved his parents, his younger brother, his hometown, and, of course, girls. By the time Hugo reached Vienna, things had changed radically since the collapse of the empire, two years earlier. Austria was now a small republic. The political atmosphere in Vienna had shifted—from the right-wing antisemitic parties to the Social Democrats. The brand-new Austrian Communist Party was popular among Hugo's friends and associates at the university, at least among the circle of mainly Jewish students who befriended him.

Hugo's relationship to Judaism, it would seem, was not then, and had never really been, more than an acknowledgment of his family's traditions. His father was not religious, although he belonged, as a matter of course, to a local Reform temple. Even though he had always been surrounded by other Jewish students back in Bielitz and continued to be closely linked to Jewish friends and colleagues in Vienna, my impression is that his friends, too, had grown up in Jewish families but not particularly religious ones, and once in Vienna they cultivated their art and their politics, not their religion.

In Vienna, Hugo assumed a new identity: he became a Communist. His girlfriend, Emily, was a seventeen-year-old typist, smart as a whip, dirt poor, but now employed by the Soviet Trade Mission. She was a Communist as was her father, a worker in a furniture factory. Hugo, too, joined the Party. Those student years in Vienna and a post-doctoral year in Paris are the subject of chapter 3.

He did not mean to be a revolutionary. He was a writer. Nothing else defined him as clearly. Already as a teenager, in Bielitz, he had been in the habit of filling notebooks with his elaborate diary entries, using shorthand. He never stopped filling those notebooks, often transcribing his quick shorthand notations into full sentences in his handsome italic script. The surviving notebooks and letters are deposited in the Hugo Huppert Archive in the Berlin Akademie der Künste, where I was able to consult them.

There is no doubt that writing was his calling. He claimed that filling his notebooks was by far his favorite activity. And, I should add, those private entries, some long and detailed, can be read as authentic testimonies, unadorned, free of the compromises required of his published writings which, of course, cannot be read as always necessarily reliable accounts of the world he lived in.

Hugo Huppert's life would have been entirely different had not external circumstances channeled his path into exile. His first years in Vienna were very difficult: hyperinflation, unemployment, food shortages. Revolution was in the air. The collapse of old empires led to armed revolts, not only in Russia, but also in the ruins of the German empire and in the Habsburg lands. Suppressed in Hungary and in Bavaria, they provoked counter-revolutionary reactions in the form of armed, dangerous militias such as the German Freikorps. The founders of the German Communist Party, Karl Liebknecht and Rosa Luxemburg, were murdered by a Freikorps gang. Liebknecht's son Helmut became a close friend of Hugo's.

In the course of a postdoctoral year of study in Paris, he found his way to the French Party headquarters and to the offices of the Party newspaper *L'Humanité*. Returning to Vienna, in 1927, he could not find work. The political situation there was just beginning to turn in the wrong direction. There were swastikas everywhere. Having married Emily, he soon followed her to Moscow.

In 1928, on the eve of the Great Depression, the Soviet Union looked good to outside observers. When the Viennese bank, the Kreditanstalt, collapsed, in 1931, while over two thousand banks in the United States followed suit, Russia would appear to many as the only healthy economy. Thousands of German workers found work there, as did American engineers, participating in the industrial boom of the Soviet Far East. Meanwhile, European and American visitors to the Soviet Union saw only progress and knew nothing about the devastating effects of forced collectivization.

In Vienna, the labor unions were under attack. By 1934, a year after Hitler's seizure of power in Germany, Socialists and Communists were persecuted, their leaders driven into exile. In Moscow, Hugo, now a member of the Russian Communist Party, wrote for Comintern publications. His first book, *Men of Siberia*, was published by the Party, both in the original German and in English translation.

In the chapters that follow Hugo's life from Vienna to Paris to Moscow to prison to war, then back to Vienna at war's end, back to Moscow, and eventually to Soviet Georgia and finally again to Vienna, I offer a portrait not only of one man but of the dangerous world he shared with other political exiles. By 1938, when Hitler took over Austria, there was no turning back. In Moscow, Stalin's staged trials and his systematic destruction of intellectuals, army officers, and Party stalwarts was reaching into the exile community. Most of the people Hugo had been working with were in danger. Some were executed; some ended up in Siberia. Hugo spent more than a year in Moscow's notorious prisons. He was lucky. He was eventually released.

He could not return to Vienna or to Bielitz. His position in Stalin's world was precarious. In 1939 the Nazi-Soviet pact allowed Hitler to attack Poland from the west, while the Red Army took over eastern regions of the country. Bielitz was in Nazi hands within hours of the German invasion. The town's Jewish citizens were doomed. Hugo's mother was no longer alive and his father was critically ill, while his brother Josef managed to take flight, together with his young wife, Lilian, just steps ahead of the armored columns. The couple found refuge in Lemberg (Lwów), which was now in Soviet hands.

And then, in June 1941, Hitler's troops invaded the Soviet-controlled parts of Poland and moved ahead into the Ukraine. Hugo, as it happened, was in Lemberg on the day of the invasion, visiting his brother. His account of the assault, written soon after he escaped the bombardments and managed to reach Moscow, is a masterful eyewitness narrative suffused with a sense of guilt: he had left behind Josef and Lilian, together with the entire Jewish community of Lemberg to face certain death.

Russia was now at war, and Hugo was a Soviet citizen and a proud member of the Soviet Communist Party. He worked in propaganda units in the uniform of the Red Army. By 1944, he was at the siege of Budapest and soon after at the liberation of Vienna. As an officer of the occupying forces with the rank of major, he enjoyed the privileges granted to the victors while at the same time fitting into the fabric of his Vienna, a city in ruins but also a city so entirely familiar that it had become his hometown. Bielitz lived only in his excellent memory. There was no longer anyone there he would know.

After four years of an exciting and productive life in Vienna, he was suddenly recalled to Moscow. He was in deep trouble, having flouted the strict regulations that forbade fraternizing with the local population. In Moscow he was removed from the Party, and Vera, his Russian wife whom he had married after Emily's death in 1923, divorced him. He could not leave the country or even correspond with anyone outside the Soviet Union for fear of being arrested again.

As luck would have it, an old Army friend, now a powerful politician in Soviet Georgia, rescued him. Hugo moved to Tbilisi with a generous contract in hand to produce a German adaptation of the Georgian national epic, a long medieval poem entitled *The Knight in the Tiger Skin*. The poem runs to more than 1,600 four-line rhyming stanzas. *Der Recke im Tigerfell* was a tour de force, published in Berlin in 1954. Two years later, rehabilitated, Hugo was allowed to return to Vienna.

He was fifty-four years old by then. He resumed his citizenship in the newly autonomous Austrian Republic and settled down to a peacetime routine. He married a local woman and led the life of a professional writer, publishing a good many volumes of poetry as well as translations, travel books, and, eventually, his autobiography in the 1970s. All his books were published in Communist East Germany.

What you discover, reading his books, especially the autobiography as well as his diaries and personal correspondence, is the price he paid in exile, in wartime, in the maelstrom of the twentieth century, for surviving against all odds. He was a nervous wreck. He had to follow orders, not only those of the Party, but also those of the established émigré politicians, those who survived the purges, the executions, and the gulag. Those men who knew him in Moscow became the ruling elite of the East German Communist State in 1945.

From the time of the purges, certainly since his own prison term in 1938, Hugo, like so many others, continued to follow the Party line—the constantly shifting Party line. The only constant was that "the Party is always right" ("Die Partei hat immer recht," in the words of what was close to being the official hymn of the Communist Party in East Germany, composed by none other than Hugo's old friend Louis Fürnberg).

Hugo spent years engaging in dutiful denunciations of the ever-growing number of "enemies of the people" while writing in Moscow's Comintern propaganda outlets, followed by a period, after his return to Vienna in 1956, of writing less strident comments in his regular articles for the East Berlin weekly *Die Weltbühne*.

Hugo had shed, at last, the permanent state of fear that had characterized his Soviet years. Shrewdly, he chose to live outside the Communist world, in Vienna, while his books were published in Communist East Germany, which supplied all his royalties and prizes. He remained a steadfast and loyal supporter of the Party. Was it convenience? Was it genuine belief? Or was it simply habit, the ingrained habit of a lifetime? Could it be that this tortured, depressive man, having watched his whole world sinking into the Nazi hell, having witnessed at close quarters the terrible depredations caused by Hitler's wars and Stalin's bloody dictatorship, simply could not consider leaving the security of the Party, the only security he had known in his adult life?

CHAPTER—ONE

THE YEAR IS 1886. ON A DUSTY COUNTRY ROAD LEADING south from the Galician salt mines of Bochnia to the pine-covered foothills of the Carpathian Mountains, an easy distance, a young man is making his way up to the Dukla Pass. His name is Abraham Huppert. He is twenty years old. His earthly possessions, in their entirety, are packed tightly in his knapsack. He has left his family, perhaps for good.

The town of Bochnia, where he has spent his entire life thus far, is situated only a few miles east of the city of Kraków. Like many Galician towns at the time, it is in large part a Jewish town. Even as late as 1886, the vast majority of the Austrian empire's Jewish subjects are still confined to Galicia, to this eastern frontier, this poverty zone north of the Carpathians, stretching from the Vistula to the Dniester River valleys. Named after the town of Halicz (or Galicz) on the Dniester, Galicia is rich in natural resources, including salt, cattle, timber, and grain. But it remains a land with miserable prospects for its inhabitants. The mass of the peasantry had ceased being unfree labor only recently, while the town-dwelling Jews were too numerous to live comfortably given the limited opportunities in trade and industry.

These Galician Jews were poor, for the most part, and their poverty was like an incurable disease. They lived on various kinds of hope: they hoped that they would be able, someday, to put more food on their table, that their Gentile neighbors would stop assaulting them, that special burdensome taxes singling them out would be removed. They hoped that their centuries-old exile in this hostile land would end and that they, or their children, or their children's children, would at last be granted the most elementary rights, that they would be able to move about freely, enjoy the protection of the law, live lives without fear, and have their dignity restored. There was no consensus among them about how such hopes might be fulfilled. There were those who lived in expectation of miracles, of prophecies realized, of a messiah bringing deliverance. Some thought in terms of a return to the Holy Land. Others dreamed of new continents, of emigration from Europe to America. And then there were those who sought salvation in more conventional quarters, closer to home, with more modest expectations. They opted, cautiously, for assimilation.

Abraham, his brother, Emmanuel, and my own grandfather, Jacob, whose precise relationship to the Hupperts of Bochnia is not quite clear to me, all belonged to this last category of dreamers. While Abraham grew up near the salt mines of Galicia, elsewhere, to the west, there were Jewish industrialists, railroad magnates, politicians, lawyers, doctors, and journalists who had been merging into the mainstream of the German-speaking middle class with considerable success. The Galicians were latecomers, but it remains true that when Abraham set off to explore the opportunities on the other side of the mountains, conditions had become optimal for leaving the East, this ancient reservation, once and for all. Without going so far as to claim that the world was prepared to embrace Galician Jews with open arms, one can at least maintain that conditions had never been so good in the past. With hindsight, one has to add: and they would never be as good again.

In their fathers' time, the mountains still stood as a barrier. Neither Jews nor Polish peasants were allowed to leave Galicia freely in those days. Kraków was still closed to Jews then, and so was Biala, the border town that marked the limit of Galician territory. Across the bridge separating Polish Biala from German Bielitz, only persons provided with proper documentation would have been allowed to enter the empire's Silesian and Moravian provinces, where Jews were not allowed to reside before the 1850s.

The coming of the railroad did more to remove barriers than any imperial edicts. From Vienna, Rothschild's Northern Railway soon reached Brünn, Bielitz, Teschen, Auschwitz, Ostrau, Kraków, and Bochnia, linking the Galician hinterland, bit by bit, with the coal mines and factories of Silesia and Moravia. The railway was to reach all the way to the Russian border, unrolling across Galicia, heading for Lemberg and Brody, and branching out to the south toward Czernowitz, the German-speaking, heavily Jewish outpost in the empire's Rumanian borderlands.

As the railroad moved eastward, Galicia was jolted out of its immobility. New laws merely ratified new circumstances. Polish peasants became free agents almost overnight because they were needed in the coal mines. Jewish townspeople began to head westward to look for work and a decent life in the cities that had been closed to their ancestors. Still, even in 1886, the Galician exodus, the flight of able-bodied and adventurous fortune seekers, was hemmed in by a number of obstacles, social and psychological in nature. The attraction of the lands to the west is easy to understand. Abraham's situation was typical. His father was a cobbler who could not make ends meet. Both Abraham and his brother, it seems, tried their hand at working in the salt mines, perhaps on the railroad, too, but the competition of the newly freed peasant labor force limited their opportunities severely. Abraham picked up seasonal work on nearby farms to round out the family's income at harvest time, but there was no future for him anywhere nearby.

In his father's time, closed horizons dictated resignation, retreat into religious observances, and satisfaction in the closeness of the traditional community. There was little chance then for escaping the centuries-old stalemate. To pick up one's knapsack and head for the hills would have been an almost unbearably fearsome option in those days. What was a young man from Bochnia, with his Orthodox upbringing, to do if he left home to wander into enemy territory, where no Jews resided? Where police officials stood in his way? How was he to navigate a safe course between the blind hatred of the Slavic peasantry and the equally ferocious contempt of the German-speaking townspeople, once past the familiar, bleak terrain of his homeland, where he could at least count, in every town, on the reassuring presence of a Jewish community?

Things had changed very fast since the 1850s. Almost all the restrictive laws had been repealed. No legal obstacles stood in Abraham's way.

No one could deny him free passage; no town could close its gates to him. There were now Jewish communities, however small, in most of the cities that had been off-limits before. In Czech and Hungarian cities, even in Vienna itself, Jews had been streaming in freely for some years from rural market towns to which they had been confined. No longer kept at arm's length like lepers, by obligatory or voluntary distinctions, such as hair style, beard, hat, caftan, and yellow badges, Jews now mixed more easily with others in this liberalized empire. Within the towns, even residential segregation gradually receded. Jewish families in provincial cities such as Teschen and Bielitz might congregate more emphatically in some neighborhoods, in the commercial center of town, for instance, but the days of the ghetto and the *Judengasse* (Jewish Street) were behind them. Not far behind, certainly within an adult's memory, but nevertheless part of a past now viewed as obsolete.

It is into this freer world that Abraham stepped as he left home. He did not have to fear open harassment or discrimination as much as he would have only a few years earlier. He did not have to register with the police along the way, nor did he have to seek lodgings in designated neighborhoods or in special segregated lodging houses; he was free to seek employment of any kind, part of the first generation of Jews endowed with full civic rights. One could even say that he belonged to a favored minority, inasmuch as he spoke German and had received a basic education. These advantages set him apart, sharply, from the mass of Poles, Czechs, Slovaks, Ruthenians, Hungarians, Croats, Serbs, Montenegrins, and others who composed the overwhelming majority of the empire's subjects. The Jews could not be considered a nationality in the Habsburg Empire. They were a minority group defined by its religion. No land belonged to them, their language was not officially recognized, but an original vocation, a special calling was theirs and theirs alone. They were the bourgeoisie-in-waiting of this immense peasant empire.

A century earlier, imperial policy had already started to single out Jewish subjects for this essential role by imposing upon them—and them alone—the obligation to attend German-language schools. In an illiterate society, Jews had always been exceptional by virtue of their almost universal male literacy. Every adult male Jew was expected to read Hebrew, for religious reasons. The unforeseen consequence of this tradition was that the Jews as a group, alone among Austrian subjects, were prepared for the tasks required of a modern nation. Forbidden to own land, kept out of most occupations, they had languished on the sidelines of an agrarian economy for centuries, cultivating the impractical book learning that was to prove useful only in modern times. Literate in Hebrew, native speakers of Yiddish as well, it was easy for them to master modern German, the language of administration, of commerce, the language of cities, of culture, of science: the language of power.

Imperial edicts had forced Jewish children, since before 1800, to attend special schools. Alone among the empire's subjects, they were subjected to compulsory schooling. The aim of this legislation, enforced only sporadically and stubbornly resisted in the Orthodox communities of Galicia, was to erase the separate identity of the Jews, to "normalize" them, to turn them into "useful citizens." Forbidding the use of Yiddish and Hebrew in commercial contracts, forcing German-language instruction and secular learning on Jewish children, together with various attempts at prohibiting the wearing of traditional dress, was designed, in the spirit of the European Enlightenment, to draw Jews out of their medieval past. Add the obligation of military service, and you had a recipe, even if it worked only fitfully, for modernization.

It is true that as long as these measures offered only obligations and no rights, they could not be very effective. In the 1860s, the old recipe started working in earnest because new laws offered rights and repudiated the police methods of the past. Jews now saw genuine opportunities ahead, opportunities that turned a German and secular education, and even military service, into training programs which could lead out of poverty toward achievable and attractive goals: careers in business or in government, the prospect of higher education and further options in, for instance, medicine, engineering, law, or journalism.

There was a price to pay for these new and glorious prospects, a price to pay for the first generation, for the founding fathers, for those who had the strength of will to break out of the traditional community, to be the first to accept the glittering bargain. The price, simply put, was expatriation. Abraham Huppert was getting ready to pay this price. With every step he took on his way to the Dukla Pass he removed himself further from his familiar universe. He was stepping out into enemy territory in a time of armistice.

Abraham was prepared for this risky venture. He had attended a German-language school for several years. In addition to his native Yiddish and the Polish with which he was also familiar, he had acquired a good command of German in school. He had learned other things as well: basic science and mathematics, history and geography, a simple but solid background in each. He was equipped, at twenty, with skills and a knowledge of the world which separated him dramatically from the vast majority of the peasants and workers he would encounter along the way.

Even so, in the course of four years of wandering, he failed to gain a foothold, to insert himself into a career. He found work in Kaschau (Košice), in construction. He put away enough money to buy a train ticket to Budapest, one of the most prosperous and fastest-growing cities within the empire, a city with a large Jewish community. He did not learn Hungarian, it seems, and he did not manage to establish himself in Budapest. Penniless, he rode a freight train to Prussian Breslau, another thriving city with a large and prosperous Jewish population. He did not make it there, either. While his brother, Emmanuel, got as far as Aachen, in the Rhineland, where he was lucky enough to learn a trade and find a wife, Abraham resigned himself to returning home when the military draft caught up with him. He was already set to present himself at the induction center when he met his future wife, Anna Reich, the daughter of an innkeeper in a village near Kraków.

Like his brother, Abraham would marry above his station. It would be surprising if it were otherwise, given the ambition, the will to succeed, which one has to imagine as the natural quality of those young men willing to brave the unfamiliar, to roam the world in search of opportunity in those empire-building days. Anna's father, Abraham Reich, was far removed from the grim stagnation of the Bochnia Hupperts. His riverside inn was well known in the region. It was called the *Stara Karczma*, the old tavern. Reich was a property owner, a not inconsiderable one. One of his three daughters was to marry an even more successful Galician Jew named Maurice Beck, who was established as a jewelry manufacturer in Paris. Abraham Reich was a man of many talents, a musician among

14

other things. He was also a Polish nationalist who revered Kościuszko, the Polish national hero. It was in Reich's inn that the future Polish chief of state Pilsudski held secret meetings of his political party.

Abraham entered a different world when he struck up his first conversation with Anna, in the summer of 1890, at her father's inn on the Vistula. Abraham was twenty-four; she was seventeen. They became engaged, but before there could be any question of marriage, Abraham had to serve three years in the army, which would prove to be a world even further removed from anything with which he was familiar. In the army, Abraham became Adolf. As he pulled on his uniform and learned to fire his weapon, he left everything familiar behind him. Sent to the southernmost frontier post in the Balkans, he spent three years in alien territory, alien far beyond anything in his experience.

Before the army years, while roaming the world, Abraham had already expatriated himself to a considerable extent. He had cut himself off from his family and hometown in those years, living among strangers beyond the reach of the Orthodox Jewish community he had grown up in and which still ruled the lives of his parents. He could hardly follow dietary restrictions in those years or attend religious services regularly. Still, there were Jewish families wherever he stopped on his way. He had the option, at least, of retreating, when he wished, back into the world he knew.

His foray into Abraham Reich's orchard was no dangerous transgression, even though Reich was a far more emancipated Jew than the Jews of Bochnia. Beer and vodka flowed from the taps in Reich's inn. The food could hardly have been kosher, and Reich's passion for things secular and Polish would surely have been viewed as strange and disquieting by the family in Bochnia. As for young and pretty Anna, she spoke a halting German, a fluent Polish, but no Yiddish at all. Anna sang and played the zither, painted delicate watercolors, and, as the Hupperts of Bochnia might have seen it, had been only partially brought up as a Jewish daughter. One could hardly picture Anna with her head shaved, wearing a wig, or bathing in a ritual bath house on her wedding day.

To Abraham's way of thinking, the Reich household must have appeared liberated, exciting, and modern when compared to his parents' world. For Abraham, now Adolf Huppert, experienced in worldly ways, had already put the shtetl behind him before he put on his uniform. He bore no visible marks announcing his origins. Smooth-shaven, short-haired, upright in his stance, speaking German and at ease with German books, skilled to an amazing degree with pen and ink and with sophisticated, literary turns of phrase in the language which had become his own, Adolf embarked, perhaps reluctantly, given his discovery of Anna Reich, on a long learning experience in the Balkans that was to expand his expatriation far beyond what he might have imagined or bargained for.

Once he had completed his basic training near Kraków, close enough to Reich's inn so that he could visit Anna on Sundays, bicycling down from Fort Krzemionki, Adolf Huppert ended up posted in the empire's newly acquired Balkan territories that had been under Turkish rule only a few years earlier, south of Ragusa, on the Adriatic. There, at the fortified post of Castelnuovo, overlooking the Bay of Cattaro, where the Imperial Navy had a base, he was to spend three years without a single leave in a setting as alien as one could imagine among other recruits gathered from the four corners of the empire, probably not a Jew among them. The battalion to which Adolf was assigned was something of a punishment unit, it seems, staffed with recalcitrant or suspect soldiers and officers.

Adolf had little in common with the soldiers in his battalion, a rough lot, few of them with any but the most basic education or even fluency in German. Adolf seems to have gotten along with his fellow soldiers anyway while keeping his own perspective, watching himself move about in this doubly hostile territory where Montenegrin bandits and guerillas took potshots at the Austrian patrols from behind the parched, boulder-strewn mountainsides. Adolf was keenly aware, as his letters to Anna show, of the absurdity of his situation, of the roles he was required to play as a soldier, as a member of an occupying force who had begun to look at the whole military enterprise with cynicism.

"I look at these veiled Muslim girls and women going past, wearing baggy trousers: I see only their eyes, sometimes very beautiful, shining eyes, the rest of their faces covered by black veils. Sometimes even the eyes are covered. They slink past us like hostile shadows. I follow them with my eyes. Not once has one of those Islamic nunlike creatures turned around," he wrote to her. And it occurred to him that he, too, had learned to cover his face with a veil of sorts, that he, too, found it necessary to hide his true feelings all day long.

> Couldn't it be said that I too, if the truth be known, that I, too, carry a veil something like theirs to hide my race? If I want to be truthful with myself, I have to confess that I do not want to be recognized, I want no one to see through me. I am an outsider here, foreign even to myself, a burglar, a murderer, without justification. No one must find out what I think and how I think here, amidst these stark, unforgiving canyons. What business have I here, a fool among fools in combat gear? I am afraid of myself and I am afraid of everyone I encounter. The veil which I carry is the same as theirs even though it is invisible. Behind it is the evidence of my flight from myself (*Eigenflucht*), of my denial of who I am (*selbstverleugnung*). I observe and I hate and I am observed and hated.[1]

Adolf had a lot of time on his hands while he was stationed at Castelnuovo. He missed Anna, of course, and everything that was familiar. He felt the strain of constant, unrelieved play-acting. What had he, the unemployed young Jewish fellow, the serious student of German literature, in common with the desperadoes in uniform and the ragged bandits on the hillsides? In his hour of need, he found refuge in books. He found several volumes of Heine and Schopenhauer at a bookseller's in Spalato, he told Anna, triumphantly:

> September has come . . . and I freeze, sometimes, deep down to my soul, but today I am as happy and I feel as fresh as a lilac bush in May: on my shelf I have two volumes of Heinrich Heine and two volumes of Arthur Schopenhauer, the *Reisebilder* and the *Französische Zustände* as well as *Die Welt als Wille und Vorstellung*. I am learning to respect the ways in which these two men manage, each in his own way, to be different, original, distinct from the crowd. I read them aloud to myself, without preconceptions, with clear eyes, and as I listen to myself, mostly outdoors, in a corner near the artillery battery, I hear, at last, a sundrenched, precise and beautiful German. For me, in my circumstances, here, this is intoxicating.

Adolf's letters sent an unmistakable message from the wilds of Montenegro. There is boredom in the background, of course, and there is a

---

1. This passage is taken from a letter to Anna quoted in Hugo's memoir, written in 1974–1975: Hugo Huppert, *Die Angelehnte Tür* (1976; reprint, Halle and Leipzig, 1982), 37 (my translation). All the other observations concerning the life of Abraham/Adolf Huppert come from the same memoir.

good deal of literary posing. The letters are often playful. Their author had to work hard, after all, at captivating his one and only but all-important reader's interest. He had to charm Anna, draw her into his exotic situation. He jokes, signing his letters "Ibrahim Effendi" (Sir Abraham), but his anguish is ever present and genuine. He has expatriated himself so thoroughly that he can no longer draw on his native language, his native experience, when he needs relief from the strangeness of his new circumstances. He confesses to being an outsider, foreign even to himself. He acknowledges that he has fled from himself, from his own. As he tries to combat this disquieting feeling of belonging nowhere, what does he do? He pulls out a sheet of luxurious Italian stationery, dips his pen into the inkwell, and writes in his calligraphic, regular, Gothic script, in his best German, which Anna will answer in Polish.

Adolf, I suspect, has no way of retreating now. He has been modernized beyond repair. Does he write to his parents in Bochnia at all? Perhaps not. His Bochnian past is already on the way to becoming a closed chapter. In later years his son Hugo, will be struck by the complete absence of photographs of his Bochnian grandparents and other relatives. Adolf's children will never see their Huppert grandparents. And here, at the age of twenty-six, at his military post, estranged equally from the primitive recruits in the barracks and the local population, alone among Christians and Muslims, Adolf thirsts not for the Bible but for German literature and philosophy. And when he does, at last, find a congenial soul in the garrison, it is in the unlikely person of a Czech lieutenant who notices that Adolf reads serious German books.

The distance created by rank notwithstanding, Adolf finds in Lieutenant Križ a suitable companion. Both men are posted at the very end of the road, far from the parade grounds of their homelands, where a friendship between an officer and a conscript would have been unthinkable. Both men are isolated. Both have a German education. And both nurse secret sympathies for the people whose land they were sent to occupy. Križ was a militant Czech nationalist who predicted the downfall of the Austrian empire. Adolf seems not far behind when he points out, for Anna's benefit, "the ugly truth in our empire."

Adolf's course was set. When he completed his tour of duty and returned to Anna, Bochnia had slipped away beyond the horizon. A quick wedding at Reich's inn, a wedding scandalous enough from an Orthodox perspective that few Hupperts would have attended it, a short honeymoon in a nearby mountain resort, and the new couple went on to settle in the town of Biala, where they knew no one but remained within reach of Anna's family. Biala, which had excluded Jews not so long before, was at the very edge of Polish-speaking Galicia. Only a bridge separated it from German-speaking Bielitz.

Honorably discharged from the military, Adolf possessed the right skills for becoming a civil servant, starting at the bottom. He passed a written examination and became a mail carrier. He would rise, slowly and predictably, in the hierarchy of the Imperial Post Office, working first in the smaller Biala post office, later in the main post office in Bielitz, where he was to be known as "der Herr Posthuppert," just as my own grandfather was known in Teschen, down the road, as "der Herr Spediteurhuppert." Both men had put their Galician youth behind them and entered the mainstream of the Austrian bourgeoisie.

Abraham had become Adolf. No word of Yiddish ever crossed his lips in his son's hearing, and any reference to his parents made Adolf uneasy, according to Hugo. Adolf, for all that, did not stop being a Jew except perhaps in Orthodox eyes. He and Anna joined a Reform congregation. They did attend religious services on the High Holy Days. They were probably among those who were jokingly referred to as "Four Day Jews": people who came to the synagogue only for the three most important Holy Days—and the emperor's birthday.

Privately, Adolf seemed to look at all religions impartially, as outward observances which had a place assigned to them by philosophy. Adolf, who supervised his sons' education, recommended Schopenhauer on religion. "Religion," wrote Schopenhauer, "is the metaphysics of the common people. We must not take it away from them and we should even show outward respect for it. To discredit religion would mean leaving them without it. A popular metaphysics fulfills a need, as does popular poetry, just as popular wisdom is contained in old sayings. Men require some sort of structure to help them interpret their lives. And this must be suited to their capacity for understanding."

In this respect, as in so many others, the Hupperts of Bielitz seem to have been entirely conventional. Heine, Schopenhauer, and Kant stood in their glass-fronted bookcases. They read the liberal newspapers of Vienna, Prague, and Budapest, above all the Vienna *Neue Freie Presse,* the newspaper of record, edited mostly by assimilated, liberal Jews, whose worldview matched that of their readers perfectly. Adolf had adopted German philosophy as his faith. He now found it difficult to maintain relations with that older community in Bochnia. It was not distance that cut him off from his origins.

He and Anna lived only a few miles away from Kraków. With the Reich family they maintained the closest of relations. Anna and the children would spend entire summers at her family home, down by the river, among the apple orchards. Bochnia is only a few miles further to the east. Adolf could have walked to Bochnia, had he wished to. But he did not. Perhaps he was no longer welcome. In any case, this remained forever a closed chapter in his life.

His brother, Emmanuel, on the contrary, in spite of traveling so much farther, made no effort to forget Galicia. He married in Germany, learned the furrier's trade, and spent most of his life in Paris, of all places, curing pelts in the overcrowded Jewish shtetl in the Marais neighborhood, rue de la Grange Batellière, speaking Yiddish and remembering the old country. It was thanks to Emmanuel that Hugo was to learn some of the bare details of his father's Galician youth. Expatriation, it seems, had nothing to do with distance. The Yiddish shtetl crossed the Atlantic and was re-created in New York, while those who chose to join the mainstream in Austria tended to cut their links to the traditional past even if they moved no farther than an hour's drive from their origins.

The twin cities of Bielitz and Biala could be described as the least adventurous choice possible for someone in Adolf's situation in 1893, a truly reasonable choice for an ex-Galician Jew whose culture and professional ambitions were modest. Adolf had not, after all, attended a Gymnasium and he had no possibility of acquiring a higher degree. He could not aspire to becoming a lawyer, a doctor, or an engineer. He turned his back on the various forms of commerce available to a man in his position once he had become linked through marriage to the Reich clan. Perhaps he did not want to owe his success to anything other than his own hard work? Or perhaps, and this may have been the determining factor, his years of expatriation, his long residence in enemy territory, taught him to avoid those customary Jewish ways of earning a living which he had learned to feel embarrassed about, given the unrelenting antisemitic campaigns which were just then reaching a crescendo.

What was tavern-keeping but getting Christian peasants drunk and keeping them in debt? What was hotel-keeping but the propagation of sin? My grandfather, Jacob Huppert, started in business keeping a tavern in nearby Friedek-Mistek. One of the Reich relatives, Anna's uncle Wilder, who had been to America, managed the Hotel City in Kraków, a sumptuous establishment staffed with young chambermaids whose morals were far from rigorous—or so it seemed to Hugo when he visited as a boy. Of course, there is no reason to think that Jewish shopkeepers, innkeepers, or hoteliers were less scrupulous than their Christian counterparts, but the perception of the Jewish businessman as an exploiter of Christian innocence was beginning to harden into a hateful stereotype propagated by antisemitic agitators. It was already so powerful, so hurtful a libel that Adolf was hardly unusual in his squeamishness. He chose to avoid any activity that could by any stretch of the imagination provoke blame in anyone's eyes. And so he opted for the civil service.

The new couple settled in a modest apartment in Biala. Adolf and Anna may have felt like pioneers, coming to live in a town where they had no relatives and stepping as strangers into a world that had been off-limits to Jewish families only forty years earlier. But in the course of those years, Biala/Bielitz had changed beyond recognition. At the beginning of the nineteenth century, the town was still dominated by an early modern workshop economy, that of the celebrated Silesian weavers whose way of life was to be destroyed by the arrival of English steam-powered looms. Those Silesian weavers were German-speaking and often Protestant, in Bielitz and Teschen and a few other communities nearby, Friedek-Mistek in particular, where my grandfather settled and where Sigmund Freud's father, another Jacob, made his living in the 1840s and 1850s.

The world of the Silesian master weavers had been in existence since the sixteenth century. In 1815, the year in which Solomon Mayer, Freiherr von Rothschild, arrived in Vienna, to serve as the principal consultant for development to the Austrian government, there were still 700 master weavers active in Bielitz and in its German suburbs of Kunzendorf and

Alexanderfeld, another 500 across the river, in Biala. There were at the time no Jews residing legally in either town, although the weavers were dependent on Jewish merchants like Jacob Freud for the import of raw wool from Galicia and Russia, and also for the sale of their finished products to the eastern markets. Jewish business agents had always played a key role in this economy, but they were kept socially at arm's length, allowed to come and go of necessity but forbidden to rent or buy a house or even spend a night in town, except with special permission and under the watchful control of the police. Rothschild himself was not able to check into a hotel in Vienna. And Jacob Freud was tolerated in Freiberg only as a visitor before the revolutions of 1848.

A new wind was blowing from the west, however, long before 1848. English machines served by Polish workmen were replacing the hand loom workshops in the 1820s. They were met with resistance at first, with riots and smashed machines, but the trend became inexorable, especially as Rothschild was building the first railroad out of Vienna, the Nordbahn, beginning in the 1830s. Soon coal, mined in nearby Witkowitz, the country estate Rothschild bought for its huge underground deposits, was linked to Vienna, to Bielitz, to Teschen, and, eventually, to Brody, Lemberg, and Czernowitz by rail. The railroad and the coal mines, western capital and technology, including English locomotives, transformed Silesia very quickly into a scaled-down Manchester, an Austrian Ruhr Valley complex.

In the course of a single generation, Austrian Silesia became one of the most densely populated and most industrialized regions in the empire. By the time Adolf settled in Biala/Bielitz, a formidable array of small factories had changed the sleepy towns into an industrial powerhouse. By 1912, there were eighty-seven textile mills in operation, thirty-six of them owned by Jews, to say nothing of the second-rank industries, including distilleries, furniture factories, paper mills, soap factories, and breweries. Bielitz acquired a new aspect in those years, its old wooden houses replaced by three-story apartment buildings built of sandstone and brick. Gas and electricity plants were built and electric streetcars were brought in, together with a profusion of new shops, new schools, churches, temples, a theater, and, of course, the imposing post office. The population nearly tripled from 7,000 to 20,000 in Bielitz alone, where

Jewish families, absent before 1848, now accounted for 3,000 inhabitants, 16 percent of the total, by 1910.

The Hupperts did not enter into an alien world. There were Jewish places of worship, Jewish schools, Jewish social clubs and organizations on hand to welcome them. It was possible, at the turn of the century, in a town like Bielitz for a Jewish family to have few, if any, relations with Gentiles in their day-to-day experience, except at the office and except for the servants who tended to be Polish peasant women. While Adolf moved in a cosmopolitan world at the post office, Anna tended to maintain relations with neighbors and shopkeepers, few of whom—landlords and tenants, grocers, pharmacists or doctors—would be strangers to her. All would be familiar kinds of people, German-speaking Jews with distant roots in Galicia.

When people like the Hupperts ventured beyond their kin and kind to maintain at least superficially cordial relations with non-Jewish neighbors, they were, on the whole, assured of a civilized reception. But something was changing, just then, in the 1890s. Twenty years earlier the social barriers had been removed voluntarily. For some time, before Adolf and Anna chose to settle there, Bielitz had been, after centuries of exclusion, a fairly welcoming sort of place for the right kind of Jewish newcomer. Not, perhaps, for the Galician Jew in caftan and sidelocks, but certainly for the kind of Jew Adolf was, the kind who could pass unnoticed and blend into the mass of the German lower bourgeoisie.

At the top of the social hierarchy, the wealthiest families, many of them Jewish, set the tone. They lived in the most attractive neighborhood surrounded by servants, amid tennis courts and carefully tended gardens. Champagne flowed freely in their costly villas. Their sons and daughters, sleek and fashionably dressed, were headed for Vienna, to the universities and eventual incorporation into the aristocracy, with an occasional baptism along the way. This cosmopolitan German-Jewish elite set the tone. It was their money and their taste that supported the opera, the concert series, and theater, all of a high standard.

All doors, for a time, were open to the new honorary Germans. This was true not only in Bielitz, but also in the larger cities, in Prague and Vienna and Budapest. On the other hand, by the time the Hupperts arrived, a counter-trend was becoming apparent. The Jewish factory owners were as glamorous as ever, the opera and the theater were doing very well, but the private clubs began to close their doors to their Jewish neighbors. This, too, was hardly a local aberration. The same hardening of lines was happening everywhere. By the time Hugo was ready to attend school, he was entering a world that sent mixed signals. On the surface, the boy was welcome, as the law required. He did not attend a Jewish school. Instead, he was enrolled in the public German schools of Biala and then in the imposing State Gymnasium in Bielitz, which was becoming a preserve of the Jewish middle class: although Jews, according to census figures, accounted for 16 percent of the town's population, they accounted for 42 percent of the student body in the Gymnasium. This did not mean that Jewish boys were made to feel at home in the classroom, where a crucifix occupied a place of honor next to the emperor's portrait and where virulently racist teachers did not mince words when they expounded on the superiority of the "white race." Hugo, in his memoir, draws a quick sketch of the history teacher, Hickl, with his catalogue of pan-German nationalist bêtes noires: the English, of course, the Americans and Negroes, to be sure, and the Chinese, the "Yellow Peril" that would destroy Europe if Kaiser Wilhelm did not rescue it. Teachers like Hickl would welcome the war in 1914 ecstatically, even while evading the draft. Not that this type of furious German nationalist was the only sort of person to be found on provincial high school staffs. There were others, quiet, liberal types like Dr. Stettner, who knew how to slip in a word or two against clerical domination and who made sympathetic comments about atheism, Buddhism, and socialism. Then there was the occasional Jew on the faculty, like Kulka, the mathematics teacher.

It was an already dangerous world Hugo was experiencing when he roamed beyond the comfortable certainties built up in his parents' private world. At home, he was growing up as a fledgling member of the liberal German Jewish middle class, which relied on the *Neue Freie Presse* and on the worldview encapsulated on Adolf's bookshelves. Was it possible to avoid contact with another reality—that of the brutal and vulgar hostility directed at Jewish fellow citizens? This, too, was reported in the newspapers, discreetly in the *Neue Freie*, in shrieking headlines in the gutter press. Not a month went by without reports of pogroms in Russia, of show trials of Jews accused of murdering innocent Christian virgins, whose blood, so the masses believed, was an indispensable ingredient in the fabrication of *Osterbrot*, "Easter bread," the unleavened bread eaten at Passover celebrations.

Hugo does not mention the famous ritual murder trials that had become the staple of the popular press throughout his childhood. Could he have avoided hearing about Jews accused of abducting Christian girls? Could he have avoided hearing about the preeminent role Jews were accused of playing in the wholesale abduction of young girls destined for South American brothels? Or the thundering denunciations that had never stopped coming from Catholic pulpits against the employment of Christian girls as servants in Jewish households? And about the riots directed at Jews, mob attacks that were commonly dismissed as "antisemitic excesses" in the jargon of the press and of the government? Is it conceivable that a precocious and sensitive boy could grow up in a town like Bielitz in the early years of the twentieth century without carrying, silently, this heavy baggage of bewildered anxiety in his head?

He could not fail to sense the way in which even an agnostic liberal like his father bowed to the inevitable in those years and turned toward Zionism, a reflexive action in self-defense. Gradually excluded in one way after another, Jews responded by creating their own separate clubs and associations. The earliest Austrian lodge of B'nai B'rith was founded in Bielitz in 1889. An association of Jewish university students was created in 1896, summer camps for Jewish children functioned as early as 1903, and Zionist clubs made their appearance in 1904. A Leopold Huppert from Bielitz was a delegate to the first Zionist Congress in Basel, in 1899.

Newspapers serving a specifically Jewish readership—some old, like the *Jüdische Volkstimme* of Brünn, some newer, like the *Selbstwehr* of Prague—reported on fresh outrages. Jews were everywhere accused of imaginary crimes and everywhere insulted and threatened. One could try to ignore all this: on the eve of the First World War, one could try to protect children from disturbing news. An obedient and well-disciplined boy could keep his observations to himself.

Hugo's protective device was a common one: in his memoirs, when he is forced to acknowledge an attack, he quickly explains it away, balancing an ugly incident with an act of kindness. Does a Christian insult him? If he must, he will remember the slight, but he will try to keep it in proportion by pointing to another Christian who does not share the mass hysteria, the Jew-hatred. This is a sensible accounting procedure. After all, no one could suspect where all this would lead. Could Hugo have suspected, in 1913, that his parents' generation would be murdered in cold blood, and that his younger brother would die in a concentration camp?

As he composes his memoirs, this lone survivor evokes a less threatening decade, when the triumphs of the founding fathers were still largely intact, when Bielitz and the Austrian empire as a whole could not yet be unequivocally viewed as enemy territory. In those years, mixed marriages were common. There would have been few families among the assimilated Jews of Silesia who could not point to at least one or two relatives or acquaintances married to a Christian. My own great aunt married the Teschen master tanner Alois Rosner, an ethnic German.

The signals, on the eve of the First World War, were still mixed. Hugo, writing sixty years later, is careful not to evoke those years with hindsight. I believe that his reconstruction of his life as a boy in Bielitz in those days is as close as one can come to a dispassionate account. He does not suppress unpleasant events entirely. He deflects them just enough to remind us how one absorbed shock after shock and registered the impact mutely, not making a big issue of it, but growing restless, gradually, and feeling less and less secure. This method works when he recalls being insulted and beaten on a soccer field by older boys. Those ruffians, he reminds us, were probably outsiders, from the rural schools. And who, when all is said and done, rescues Hugo and tends to his wounds? Angelic creatures, young women from the Catholic noviate whose garden borders the field where he was assaulted.

In the one instance where he actually evokes the ideological frenzy of the time, the fanatical hatred of the "inferior races" which was spreading throughout Europe like a cancer, he manages to redirect this almost electrical force, to ground it, so that it touches him only indirectly. The year is 1913, he is eleven years old, and he meets the daughters of the widow Palluch. The late Mr. Palluch had worked in the post office and Anna, at her husband's suggestion, makes a courtesy visit to the Palluch household, a rare foray beyond the range of her normal social relations, since the Palluchs are not Jewish. The memory of this visit to the Palluch household remains rooted deep in Hugo's memory. When he recalls this episode, as an old man, his pen suddenly takes off, he becomes lyrical and rhapsodic, evoking a feverish moment of luscious sexuality.

He recalls arriving at the drab apartment building where Mrs. Palluch and her daughters live in straightened circumstances, in two rented rooms on the third floor. The building stood on a sober square, remarkable only for its statue of St. John, which was traditionally decorated with garlands of flowers at Easter. A Christian setting, bare and impoverished, or so it may appear to the visitor's eyes as he approaches the building. In back, however, what a miracle! exclaims Hugo. Behind the drab façade it presents to the world, the building hides a luxuriant garden planted with a wealth of lettuce, carrots, parsley, beans, even asparagus. This kitchen garden, which Hugo remembers with much emotion, borders on open fields. Taken together, this landscape of the St. John's neighborhood in Biala remains, for Hugo, the ideal landscape, the source of his sense of the familiar, of the native, of everything conjured up by the word *Heimat*, home.

No doubt this has to do with the rush of feelings set loose in the boy by the Palluch girls, Minka and Antschi, blond and flirtatious, who take the younger boy under their wing. The games they play with him are provocative. Minka displays her charms with studied insouciance, pulling sky-blue panties trimmed with lace out of her dresser, while Antschi, hot from running around, sits down to remove her black stockings. Hugo catches his breath as he observes the "gazelle-like" girls. He can't help staring at their hard little breasts. He feels clumsy, awkward, ordinary, confronted with their beauty, with the grace of their movements. He is overwhelmed by a feeling of awe as he contemplates the girls, whom he sees as supremely natural presences as much at home in this setting as the plants thriving in their garden.

The girls, he notes, though they are not twins, are so much alike, with their straw-colored hair, their green eyes, their perfect white teeth, that he is overcome by a sense of collusion between them. They not only look alike, they seem to obey a common, mysterious impulse. They belong together so absolutely and they are so totally and naturally part of the setting, which includes the smells of their room and the fragrant garden, that the boy feels like an outsider; he stands there, enveloped in this enchantment, experiencing a feeling of silent harmony almost painful in its intensity.

He is in love, but not with either Minka or Antschi, but indifferently with both. For the duration of one hot summer, Hugo can think of nothing else. The Palluch girls represent a "magical harmony" for him, a foreign world that exerts an irresistible, magnetic pull. He feels himself drawn into it, even while he is aware that he remains an outsider. The strength of these feelings, experienced in 1913, is enormous, still uneroded in 1974. The attraction will remain alive, even though his acquaintance with the girls will end abruptly, a few weeks after it began. The end of this emotional affair will be brought about by a single phrase, by mere words, pronounced by Minka on a hot summer afternoon, as she kneels in the sunshine, half-undressed, next to her mother, on the sundeck. Those fateful words were not even addressed to Hugo.

The circumstances, as Hugo tells it, are the following: that day he comes to visit, as usual, with his mother. There is no answer at the Palluchs' door.

"They are upstairs, on the roof," says an elderly neighbor. "Sunbathing."

Anna and Hugo climb up to the roof, where, sure enough, Mrs. Palluch and her daughters are stretched out, half-naked, sunbathing. Adding to the exotic sight is the presence of an elderly Chinese gentleman, the most unusual tenant of the building, who is also enjoying the sunshine, in the company of his pet monkey. He is described as a refugee, polite, friendly, and fond of children. Mrs. Palluch has nothing against him, as she explains, in her most tolerant manner. Why Mr. Kwang Tsaiti is living in Biala, she does not know. (Trust Hugo to know the name of a man he saw once, in 1913. He could also tell you with authority how to get to the Palluchs' house.)

"Perhaps he is a political refugee?" remarks Anna. "That is sort of interesting."

"Really," says Mrs. Palluch, "as the widow of an imperial civil servant I can hardly excuse a revolutionary, and, in any case, I can hardly be expected to take an interest in his fate. He is not a Christian, after all. He is a heathen."

"My dear Mrs. Palluch," says Anna, "Buddhists are not heathen. They follow an ancient faith, they do not worship idols, and as for the shape of their eyes and of their cheekbones, this does not seem to me any worse than our own features."

Mrs. Palluch appears shocked at Anna's appeal for universal brotherhood. She stares at her in surprise. It is at this point that Minka gets up on her knees, and in this ravishing pose asks: "But are we not the white race?"

Those words have the effect of a cold shower, even sixty years later. Abruptly, Hugo pulls away from his reverie and remarks that such talk was not harmless in 1913.

The contempt for the Chinese naively expressed by a fourteen-year-old girl, on the rooftop in Biala that summer, was a turning point for Hugo. It was a dose of poison. The sweet infatuation was over. "His pride," says Hugo of his younger self, "helped him overcome his sorrow." To be sure, Minka's remark was not directed at him. Nor was there anything malicious about it. She had nothing against Kwang. She was merely repeating a cliché found in every illustrated magazine, a banality. But Hugo took it personally. He came to the defense of Kwang, just as his father had, twenty years earlier, when he described the Muslims he had been sent to pacify.

In both cases, one does not have to look very far to find the source of his reaction. Adolf, the Austrian infantryman, understood clearly enough that he was in no position to dismiss the local Muslims as an inferior race. He could not adopt the outlook of the "white race," of which he felt himself to be, at best, an honorary member, on probation. Hugo's yearning to belong, his helpless admiration of Minka and Antschi, was more than an early manifestation of puberty. He did not fall in love with a girl: he was swept off his feet by a deeper longing, of which Minka and Antschi were interchangeable manifestations.

When he remarks that Minka's question was not harmless in 1913, the harm he has in mind is not the harm inflicted on Chinese refugees, but on Jews. Minka would not ever be in a position to harm Chinese, but one can easily picture her and her sister standing at the roadside, near St. John's square, years later, waving as German tanks marked with swastikas rolled into Biala. Minka's naive question, as Hugo hears it, has the strength of a poisoned dart. I cannot vouch for the accuracy of Hugo's recollections, but the poison lodged under his skin all the same. As an old man, he still avoids saying directly why he was hurt that day on the roof. He pretends that it was the offense given to Mr. Kwang that made further contact with the Palluch family impossible.

But any one of his readers, I should think, can see what is really going on from the moment he singles out St. John's square as the Garden of Eden where he lost his innocence. The statue wreathed in green foliage and flowers at Easter time sticks in his mind, marking the entrance into Christian territory. The garden in back of the Palluchs' tenement, this Christian garden, provokes feelings so strong in the young boy's mind that he will, forever, embed this scene in his imagination as his true and desired natural setting, his *Heimat*. What an extravagant reaction to a kitchen garden, even allowing for the charming girls who are not clearly separated from the botanical context. They belong, the girls as much as the plants. Hugo does not belong. He yearns to belong, but he discovers that this vision of paradise is a fleeting vision bound to elude his grasp.

That intense encounter on the sundeck, as preserved in the old poet's memory, is a fine instance of the delicacy with which the relationship between Jews and Christians had to be handled: in this instance, there is no reference to Jews at all. Mrs. Palluch has been receiving Mrs. Huppert's visits for some time and the children have played together on those occasions. Poor Mrs. Palluch knows better than to make antisemitic remarks to her visitor's face. She has nothing against Mrs. Huppert; on the contrary, she welcomes her visits. She has nothing against Kwang, either. To say that she cannot be expected to take an active interest in someone who is not a Christian is just a banal statement. No wonder Mrs. Palluch's jaw drops in surprise when Anna goes on the attack: Buddhists are not heathen! For Mrs. Palluch there are only two kinds of people, Christians and heathen. She probably does not mean much with her statement about the Chinese. So why does Anna go on so, trying to convince her that Buddhists are not heathen because theirs is an ancient faith and they believe in only one God?

The answer, which may or may not have occurred to Mrs. Palluch, is that Anna was not really thinking about Buddhists, but about Jews.

And when Minka rises to shift the ground away from religion to race, why is Hugo so deeply hurt? He decides never to see the girls again, a decision that causes him deep sorrow. But, he tells us, his "pride helped him overcome his sorrow." Pride in what, exactly? Pride in defending the Chinese? No, in staying away from where you are not wanted, pride in overcoming the temptation represented by the sun-tanned blond natives in their garden.

There are unspoken, unspeakable fears and desires just barely below the surface of these memories. Fitted into the broader context of Jewish-Christian relations in the early years of the twentieth century, they can be understood by noting the obscene whispers and shouts rising up from the collective unconscious of ignorant, superstitious, and angry people. There were others, too, decent people secure enough to resist the demonic appeals of the agitators. But the tide was washing in, shrewdly channeled by politicians who had much to gain from arousing the mob. By the time Hugo lost his innocence, relations between Christians and Jews had been systematically and openly poisoned in the Austrian empire. Still provided with legal equality, still protected by the emperor, Austrian Jews, more successful than ever, more in the public eye, were, at the same time, put on the defensive.

CHAPTER—TWO

IT WOULD HAVE BEEN DIFFICULT, IN 1913, TO IGNORE THE charges leveled against Jews. Such charges had become so common, so frequently repeated, so ubiquitous, that they were achieving a respectability of sorts. The liberal imagination, meanwhile, was dazzled by the progress of legislation and hopeful about the eventual disappearance of irrational behavior in politics. The liberal scenario was especially dear to the empire's Jewish population. There is no denying that liberal legislation had produced fundamental changes. The second half of the nineteenth century was a time of unprecedented freedom and security for Austrian Jews. For someone born in a real ghetto, where the gates were closed at night and thousands of pale and sickly people crowded into a one-street slum, the reforms were tangible and of a heroic quality.

The revolution of 1848 had been greeted with heartfelt optimism by Jewish editorialists: "Words are free at last, ideas are free! Even we need no longer suffer quietly all the injuries that have oppressed and humiliated us for so many years. We can look forward, in Austria, to a finer, to a better future." This is the tone of the editorial on March 24, 1848, in the pages of the *Österreichisches Zentral Organ für Glaubensfreiheit*.

But the tone changed very quickly, as reports of "excesses" reached the editors. In Vienna, posters carrying libelous attacks against Jews appeared on many street corners in July. Even in peaceful Teschen, "where Jews and Christians had lived in harmony," there was a sudden increase of official actions and of harassment of Jewish inhabitants (July 2, 1848). In Prague and other cities mobs continued to pursue Jews. It did not take long for Jewish journalists in Vienna to change their tune. Already on May 6, an editorial was headlined: "Let us emigrate to America." After a sober analysis of the new wave of mob actions, the editorialist concluded: "Things look worse than ever."

Not a year will go by after that without reports of riots in one town or another. Major outbreaks of violence, requiring the intervention of the military, were reported in 1861 in Prague, where the final tally was 1,312 broken windows. Government officials acknowledged the obvious in their reports: "You simply cannot shake the persuasion of the lower classes which is that the Jews are guilty whenever calamity strikes, whenever something goes wrong." Something went wrong, of course, almost all the time.

Those were not quiet years for the great mass of the population. The transition from rural serfdom to industrial revolution was a wrenching experience. Peasants and working men throughout the empire were disoriented and hurt as they found themselves working under atrocious conditions in factories and mines, just to keep food on the table. At the same time, liberal legislation now allowed previously unprintable opinions to come freely to the surface. Posters and pamphlets called for the extermination of Jews: "This is a war against the Jews and they must all be killed, we must bathe in Jewish blood," screamed posters in the streets of Prague during the summer of 1866. In 1870, the sentiment was much the same: "Let's get the Jews, let's strangle them, let's hang them, let's drown them, let's shoot them."

Things went from bad to worse as voting rights were extended and liberal deputies lost their majority in parliament. By 1882, the calls for mass murder were no longer confined to shadowy pamphlets. Anti-semitism was on its way to respectability. Politicians addressed crowds at mass rallies, explaining that there is no problem in the empire except "the Jewish problem." They called openly for the abolition of the laws that had led to Jewish emancipation. In the meantime, in Bohemia they called for boycotts of Jewish merchants under the popular slogan "Shop only in Christian shops."

Czech, Hungarian, and German antisemites began to make common cause in the early 1880s as they discovered the most successful strategy of all: reviving the medieval accusation of ritual murder and its exploitation in courts of law, resulting in sensational press coverage. The modern reader, unless he lives in a Muslim-majority country, may blink in disbelief when reading about ritual murder accusations made not in the thirteenth century, but in the late nineteenth and twentieth centuries. These were not isolated instances. Such accusations were now common. A number of actual trials resulted. And there was even an actual conviction. Unrelenting efforts were made to keep the topic of ritual murder alive.

This would seem to be such unlikely stuff. Such accusations belong to the medieval past, don't they? This would be a reasonable reaction in the mind of the modern reader—unless he had made it a point to study the Austrian press of that time. Just how improbable these accusations appear to the modern reader can be seen in a passage of Henri Louis de La Grange's authoritative biography of the composer Gustav Mahler.La Grange was a meticulous scholar who was by no means unacquainted with the historical context of Mahler's life. He was no armchair historian. He traveled to Mahler's birthplace, his little *Heimat*, the town of Iglau (Jichlava), in Bohemia, on the road from Vienna to Prague. Iglau was not very different from Bielitz: another German-speaking textile town surrounded by Czech-speaking villages. Gustav Mahler grew up in a Jewish family in Iglau. His father, a rural tavern keeper, took the opportunity of the new freedom to move his family and his business into Iglau, which had, before 1848, excluded Jews.

La Grange read the Iglau newspaper to get a sense of what it was like to grow up in this town in the 1860s and 1870s. He stopped reading too soon. Had he continued to follow local history right up to 1900 and beyond, he would have received a different impression. By then, Mahler was baptized, married, and a world famous conductor. It is only in the spirit of irony that La Grange refers, in passing, to something he read about, vaguely, namely that ritual murder accusations were directed at a young Jewish man in the village of Polná, within walking distance of Iglau. To think that in the very vicinity of the town where Mahler's genius was nurtured, "it was still possible for a Jew to be accused of the ritual murder of a Christian child as recently as the eighteenth century!" exclaims La Grange.

This is a very telling example of what happens when you try to take in something that is so utterly foreign to your own conception of reality that you simply push the information away. La Grange heard about, or read about, the Polná ritual murder case, which took place, not in the eighteenth century, but in 1900. It was not just an accusation: there was a trial—and a conviction. The Polná ritual murder case played out in the press as much as did the Dreyfus Affair in France. To put the matter in its proper context, one has to review the history of mass violence against Jews from the moment of their legal emancipation.

One could claim that there were no pogroms in the Austrian empire. There was plenty of mob violence, but at least no violence encouraged by the government. There were riots, there was window smashing and looting, but few fatalities. Statistically speaking, Austrian Jews had nothing to complain about, one might say, compared to what was happening in Russia. There were calls for their murder, their humiliation, their extinction, true enough, but they were empty threats. The scare tactics of nationalist politicians could be dismissed as the antics of half-crazy exhibitionists. But the fact is that the appeal of Jew-hatred, far from diminishing, was becoming ever more effective in the years leading up to the calamity of 1914.

A milestone in the history of this frenzied mass phenomenon was the ritual murder case in the Hungarian village of Tiszaeszlár, in the spring of 1882. In this godforsaken place the ancient pathologies of the illiterate, kept alive by priests, were propelled into the limelight by politicians and journalists adept at exploiting the nightmares of the masses. All at once, old folk memories, the endemic Jew-hatred of peasants and the publicity-hungry antisemitism of urban professionals, were all brought together. In the background was the memory of a ritual murder trial that had resulted in a death sentence almost a century earlier, in 1790.

Now, in 1881, especially in Budapest, Jews were reaching prominence in the universities, in journalism, in literature, in law, and in most professions. In reaction to this trend, some reckless politicians had already stirred up mobs of students to the point of attacking Jews in the streets. They issued calls for the expulsion of Jewish students, and, more generally, for the cancellation of civil rights for Jews. None of these provocations achieved the kind of press coverage that only a truly sensational case could trigger. What was needed was a mixture of sex, blood, and magic. This is what the agitators found in Tiszaeszlár.

This village of some 2,700 Christian inhabitants was also home to twenty-five Jewish families. On April 1, 1882, seven unknown Jews appeared in the village. On the same day, a young girl disappeared. It was a classic setting for rumors to get started. The lost girl's distraught mother almost immediately thought of the foreign Jews and lodged a complaint. The memory of the 1790 trial was still alive, both among some Christians and the local Jewish families. This being 1882, Jews could not simply be rounded up without some evidence. The "evidence" gradually came to light in the weeks following the girl's disappearance.

At the center of the emotionally charged events was the family of Joseph Scharf, a Jewish cobbler and farm laborer in whose house the foreign Jews were staying. There was, of course, a simple explanation for the arrival of those Jews: three of them had arrived to look for a job. The tiny, impoverished congregation had put out a call for a kosher butcher. By chance, four Jewish beggars arrived on the same day. Scharf, a dutiful, pious man, invited the destitute Jews to eat at his house. He also interviewed the three candidates for the position of ritual butcher.

From the perspective of Scharf's neighbors, there was something strange and certainly out of the ordinary in the private meetings held in the synagogue and in Scharf's home on the very day of the girl's disappearance. It was almost inevitable that the girl's mother and some others should point to the visiting Jews as suspects. Even Scharf seems to have been uneasy. He, too, must have been struck by how these coincidences might look to simple peasants who believed, as firmly as ever, in the dangerous machinations of Jews. It was Passover time, and Easter time. The local Catholic priest went out of his way to stoke those fears. Had not a Jew been sentenced to death by a court of law for such a crime?

There was probably some hushed and anguished talk that night at the Scharf family home. The next day, eight-year-old Samuel Scharf announced, while playing with a twelve-year-old girl, a Christian neighbor, that he knew what happened to Esther, the missing girl: she was cut up by the butcher. Some days later, the boy was heard shouting, in anger: "Just for that I won't tell you what my father did to that Magyar girl."

The cat was out of the bag! The priest published an article in a Catholic newspaper, insisting that a ritual murder had taken place in his village. The Scharf boy's heated declarations were now seized upon to start a police inquiry. The man appointed to be in charge of it, a virulent antisemite, descended upon the village, determined to convict a Jew. The members of the Scharf family were arrested. The synagogue was searched. Other local Jews were also questioned and some were arrested. The Scharf boy was interrogated, but he was not an ideal witness. His older brother, Maurice, on the other hand, an impressionable adolescent, was taken away, beaten, and threatened until he signed a confession. Confronted with the three kosher butchers, who had also been arrested, Maurice identified one of them as Esther's murderer. This sensational confrontation happened on May 23, in front of the prosecutor and the equally antisemitic judge. The next day the news was leaked to an antisemitic newspaper in Budapest.

The man accused of the murder, S. Schwarz, was a thirty-seven-year-old father of three, an intelligent man, dirt poor, like the other participants in the drama. He had no police record. He also had a solid alibi, but the case went forward anyway, lifted into prominence by a handful of journalists and politicians. Esther, the missing girl, achieved posthumous fame. She was celebrated as a victim of the Jews, in song and story. Her picture was published in the papers and an enlarged copy of it presided over the first meeting of the International Anti-Jewish Congress held in the city of Dresden in September of that year.

The trial began on June 19, 1883, in the courthouse of the county seat where the 1790 trial had been staged. (In that ancient event, the death sentence was pronounced, although the supposed victim eventually turned up alive.) The modern trial was not allowed to proceed in obscurity. Public opinion had been stirred up into a frenzy. The trial, however, was disappointing to the crowds. To the agitators, that did not matter. What mattered to them was the presence of the international press corps.

The verdict was "not guilty." Esther's body eventually turned up. Schwarz's innocence was indisputable, but the politicians were achieving their aim. During the trial, dangerous mobs pressed against the accused and their defense lawyer. After the verdict, the Scharfs had to be spirited away to Budapest. Riots erupted for several months, Jews were assaulted, their homes attacked. Stores were looted, synagogues vandalized, cemeteries desecrated. In the memories of simple folk, the trial and the verdict played no part, but "the murder of Esther by the Jews" was evoked with great feeling.

The lesson that professional antisemites drew from the Hungarian trial was that the wildest accusations, even if they were dismissed in court, were likely to be of great profit to them. Nothing, short of all-out war, did so much for the trashy press as accusations leveled against Jews. And of those accusations, none worked greater miracles in the circulation departments than those that involved crimes against Christian virgins. Editors who specialized in antisemitism followed every possible trail. No report of a missing girl child was overlooked, no complaints from servant girls against Jewish employers were ignored. Again and again, the antisemitic press sought to create a big hit on the model of Tiszaeszlár, but most went nowhere when no witnesses could be found to corroborate rumors.

A good case in point is one of those innumerable ritual murder accusations fabricated by Catholic priests that provided sensational headlines at Easter time in 1913, just a few weeks before Hugo Huppert came face to face with the somber side of life on that rooftop sundeck in Biala. This particular news item looked promising at first. It was carried by many newspapers, not just the specialized rags. Hugo could have hardly avoided hearing about it. It involved the disappearance of Marie Pavlik in the Czech city of Kolín. Marie's employers, the Weissberger family, were Jewish. The person who started the rumor was Marie's catechism teacher, Father Hrachovsky, who was well known as an antisemitic agitator. Hrachovsky's accusations were taken seriously in a town that had a long history of popular agitation against its Jewish citizens.

Unfortunately for Father Hrachovsky, and for the newspaper men and politicians poised for a replay of the Hungarian event, the Kolín case collapsed quickly. Marie's body was found in the Elbe River. Witnesses had seen her standing on a bridge, alone, leaning against the parapet, on the night of her disappearance. The coroner's verdict was suicide. As for the circumstances leading up to Marie's drowning, they were sordid. It seems that Father Hrachovsky had secretly been her lover and that she had found herself pregnant and desperately alone.

In the wake of the sensational events in Tiszaeszlár, Czech political operatives met with Hungarian antisemitic propagandists and declared "a crusade against modern Jewry." In the summer of 1883 the liberals lost their majority in the Bohemian regional parliament. From that moment the police records document a rise in violence directed against Jews in the streets of Prague and especially in taverns. Explosives were now more frequently confiscated. Windows were being smashed, anonymous threats surfaced ever more frequently, and Czech politicians started fishing in troubled waters. Klofač, the editor of the nationalist newspaper *Národny Listy,* and Baxa, the future mayor of Prague, were especially adept at creating anti-Jewish happenings.

In April 1897, Klofač addressed the workers striking at the Werfel shoe factories, whipping them into an antisemitic frenzy. From factory strikes directed at Jewish owners to consumer boycotts, a wide range of strategies for intimidation was available. In December of that year Jews were, once again, attacked in the streets of Prague. The violence and the scale of the attacks required the intervention of the military and the imposition of martial law. There was plunder and there were beatings, but no one was killed. In Vienna, elected officials were openly calling for mass murder.

The wholesale murder of Jews in central Europe was bandied about. Even the *Neue Freie Presse,* whose habitual strategy was denial, could not help acknowledging, obliquely, that there was talk of mass murder. The topic popped up suddenly in the course of an interview with Bismarck, published posthumously on January 4, 1898, in the wake of the Prague "excesses." Bismarck asked his interviewer, "How do the antisemitic political parties propose to get rid of all the Jews?" This was indeed the question to which no one had the answer. Quite aside from the fact that the presence of Jews in German lands was not without its positive side, Bismarck pointed out, "they add a certain *mousseux,*" a champagne-like sparkle to an otherwise dull society. Should they be exiled once again as they were in the Middle Ages? Hardly a feasible plan in the modern world, opined Bismarck. Should they be killed? Surely even the most rabid antisemites hardly dare suggest "a St. Bartholomew's Day massacre or a Sicilian Vespers"—a nationwide, concerted, sudden, all-out slaughter?

When Bismarck gave that interview, it may still have been true that no one had gone quite as far, not in public, not for attribution, not in an official forum. But in the course of the year 1899, the rhetoric of the antisemites reached its ultimate level, shedding all semblance of inhibition, whether in public, on the record, in debates in the Austrian parliament, or in the Viennese city council. Those debates were published verbatim in the *Neue Freie Presse* and, with a different slant, in the right-wing nationalist press. The public could now appreciate how quickly the calls for murder had risen from the gutter to the backbenches of parliament.

An ordinary reader of the Viennese press, someone like Adolf Huppert in Bielitz or Jacob Huppert in Teschen, could hardly fail to notice the acceleration of the process. Insults of the sort that were, no doubt, common in the backrooms of taverns at closing time were now published as a matter of course and attributed to elected officials. It is true that the deputies whose words were quoted tended to belong to a marginal group, mainly the followers of Schönerer, whose main theme was antisemitism. Those men were obvious louts playing to the gallery. Even Karl Lueger, Vienna's mayor, whose popularity rested in large part on his own antisemitic appeal, was forced to restrain Schönerer's followers, whose sole contribution to debates was to heckle, shout, and provoke.

In March 1899, at a meeting of Schönerer's group, screaming diatribes against "international Jewry" were greeted with hoarse shouts of "Sieg Heil!" You might say that this kind of behavior was to be found only within the circles of the extremists, even though it was reported in the *Neue Freie* (March 27, 1899). The same provocateurs, however, began to speak up at meetings of the Lower Austrian parliament: "That's right, the alien bodies must be removed. Out with the Jews! Let's drive out the Jews for good" (March 29). The tension increased as news of Czech workers' strikes and anti-Jewish rioting reached the press in April.

In the Bohemian town of Náchod, where workers were striking against Jacob Pick and other Jewish textile manufacturers, the rioting reached fever pitch when one of the factory owners was spotted by the crowd, followed by shouts of "Strike him! Kill him! One Jew is a worse thief than another!" The mob attacked the man while ordinary townspeople quietly stood by, offering no assistance. The police did not intervene. Encouraged by what they assumed to be the quiet complicity of the bystanders, the strikers moved on to the central square. The Pick family resided there. Around 6 PM, the crowd started smashing windows, doors, and chandeliers. An eyewitness observed "an awful screaming and howling" coming from the crowd, which began systematically destroying anything remotely connected with their Jewish neighbors.

Having smashed windows in the town's main square, the mob turned into the Steingasse, the main shopping street, where they broke into a Jewish-owned bakery, stole the money from the cash register, and calmly looted the shop for some two hours without being disturbed. They even made their way up to the first floor, above the bakery, where an elderly Jewish widow lived in a furnished room. They smashed the furniture and threw it into the street. All the while, mobs streamed down the Steingasse, destroying other Jewish-owned shops. The plundered goods were piled up in the street and the looting went on, in a holiday atmosphere and to the accompaniment of a harmonica, until three o'clock in the morning. The authorities did not intervene. "The Jews remain totally unprotected," observed a reporter.

The riot in Náchod was not spontaneous. Professional agitators were passing out leaflets. They harangued the crowd and suggested the looting of Jewish shops. Christian-owned shops were left scrupulously alone. Apparently, the event was advertised in the surrounding villages, because peasants began arriving in the course of the evening with horse-drawn carts to scoop up as much of the plunder as they could. "And all the time, the upstanding citizens of Náchod strolled along the Steingasse, laughing uproariously."

Soon after the reports of the looting in Náchod, the astounded liberal reading public received the first news of the ritual murder rumors coming from Polná. This would become the *cause célèbre* several politicians had been waiting for. The Polná case was talked about everywhere. Its impact would dwarf that of the Hungarian trial.

Polná was a rural market town of some 5,000 inhabitants, of whom about 500 were Jewish. Historically, Polná had been a satellite of the sizeable industrial town of Iglau. When the Jews of Iglau were driven out in the sixteenth century, some took refuge in Polná, where they were protected by Czech landowners. The Jewish community in Polná lived in a segregated part of the small town, itself hardly more than a large village. After the emancipation decrees of 1848, the Jewish families of Polná could move to Iglau or even Prague or Vienna. In 1899 there was no legal segregation, but Polná's Jewish families tended to remain in their own neighborhood. The place of those who moved on to Iglau or elsewhere was taken, typically, by poor rural Jews coming from the East.

On April 7, 1899, the body of a nineteen-year-old girl, Agnes Hruza, was found in the nearby woods. The girl must have been waylaid on her way home from work. Her murder appeared to have been sexually motivated. Almost immediately, rumors pointed to a likely suspect: Leopold Hilsner. He was considered likely because he was a Jew and a misfit, a twenty-three-year-old rather stupid idler who was known to spend a lot of time hanging out in the Březina woods, the site of the murder. A further connection that seemed suspicious is that Hilsner lived, together with his widowed mother, in the basement of the German Jewish school, right next to the workshop where Agnes was employed as a seamstress. The local gendarme, Klenoveč, followed up those leads. He visited the Hilsners' basement lodgings, found nothing, arrested Hilsner anyway, interrogated him, and confronted him with a witness. This witness, Mrs. Vomela, was a neighbor of Agnes's family. She happened to be walking past the murder site at about the right time. Although she heard nothing and did not see Agnes, she did see a young man whom she did not recognize and who pursued her. When confronted with Hilsner, she failed to identify him as the man in the woods. Hilsner was released.

The matter might have ended right there. At least two suspects more likely than Hilsner had been identified, especially Karl Janda, a deranged young man who had been in Polná that day and who was picked up and interned in an insane asylum in Prague, shortly after the discovery of

Agnes's body. The police knew about Janda, who gave a formal deposition on April 21. It seems that Janda was not only present in Polná on April 7, but that his clothes carried marks of both blood and semen. He may have been the stranger whom Mrs. Vomela saw, but he was never confronted with her. That particular trail of inquiry was simply allowed to drop when the people of Polná began to demonstrate their conviction that only Jews could be responsible for the heinous crime.

A mob of some 300 assembled in Polná on April 4. Soon rumors about a ritual murder spread beyond the immediate vicinity and reached a part-time Czech newspaper employee who, like many in the press, specialized in antisemitic propaganda, a man called Hušek who had been looking for an opportunity of this sort for years. He had spent fourteen days in jail, six years earlier, for propagating a false rumor about a ritual murder.

As soon as Hušek heard about the Polná murder, within a week of the body's discovery, he dashed off a letter to a colleague conveying the essentials of the charge that might be fabricated.

The clumsy but sober police inquiry did not focus so much on Hilsner as it did on the victim's brother, a stone mason with a reputation for violence. A mason's apron had been found near Agnes's body. There was a history of violence in the Hruza family. The father, an unstable man, had been murdered some time ago and his body had also been found in the woods. Hilsner, meanwhile, remained a suspect but not a prime one, until the police and the prosecutor's office simply lost their composure when the mob, the press, the Catholic clergy, and the politicians began whipping up public opinion to an unprecedented frenzy.

After so many false starts, so many false denunciations, including the published rumor at Easter time the preceding year of a young girl's body found in a box in the Bielitz train station, here, at last, was a case one could sink one's teeth into. A real body, a rustic population more than ready to believe the ritual murder charge, a local clergy working overtime to accuse Jews, a local mayor won over to the antisemites' cause! Soon the celebrities of the antisemitic circuit began arriving in Polná and in Písek, the county seat where the trial was likely to take place.

The hero of Polná was the lawyer and politician Karel Baxa, who would eventually be propelled into high office by the case's notoriety. Baxa arrived without being invited and offered to represent the Hruza family in court. He made a number of inflammatory speeches, accusing Hilsner of murder to the acclaim of the crowds, the press, and the clergy. The trial, in September, was quick. Hilsner was convicted in five days and Baxa was carried off in triumph. The verdict, however, was annulled on appeal. A new trial was set for November 1900, and Hilsner was convicted again.

The prosecution did not openly treat the case as a ritual murder, but Hilsner was sentenced to death. The violence of the crowds now spilled over into the highest reaches of political life. The events at Polná, like the riots in Náchod, sent danger signals to the organized Jewish community. The Austrian Jewish Union recognized that Náchod and Polná were links in a chain and sent a delegation to seek assurances from the prime minister. But the assault continued unabated in every province. Rioting workers in the Galician industrial center of Lemberg attacked Jewish shops. In Horitz (Hořice), threats were made and a repetition of the Nachód riots was feared.

Hilsner's conviction and sentencing were celebrated widely in a carnival atmosphere. Postcards were sold at county fairs, purporting to show Agnes's mutilated body. Simple rhymes kept the crime attributed to Hilsner in the public eye ("Oh God, Hilsner killed a pretty Christian girl"). Cheap plaster busts of Hilsner were sold in carnival booths. And, as was to be expected, copycat denunciations abounded, including one from Náchod, involving another girl's disappearance. This time a witness actually came forward to claim he saw Jews killing the girl. The corpse turned up in the river and the "witness" was convicted of false testimony.

There were a few men in positions of power who refused to capitulate to mass hysteria. The most effective was T. G. Masaryk, the Prague professor who would eventually head the independent Czechoslovak Republic after the war. Masaryk was practically the only Czech public figure who spoke out in Hilsner's defense and asked for a reopening of the case. It took a great deal of courage to speak up for reason in Prague or Vienna in 1900. Masaryk faced rioting students. For a political leader there was nothing to be gained by defending Jewish citizens in 1900.

Among the most direct beneficiaries of the Polná case were the Catholic clerics, who exploited the accompanying frenzy. A particularly telling example is provided by the inflammatory speech given by Bishop Brynych, who headed the local diocese. He spoke at a mass meeting and his speech was published in the diocesan newsletter at the height of the agitation, after Hilsner's first conviction and in anticipation of a new trial.

The bishop's theme was blood. The blood of the Jews had been spilled eighteen centuries earlier at the time of the destruction of the Temple in Jerusalem, an event evoked with enthusiasm in such a way that the bishop's audience was expected to applaud the massacre as just punishment for those who were said to have killed their god.

"So many of the Jews were killed on this occasion that their blood filled all the streets and ditches and it flowed like a stream down the steps of the Temple," Brynych noted. He added, erroneously, that this bloodbath took place on the High Holy Days and informed his listeners that "ever since, a curse lies on this people without Fatherland or King, without altar or priests, hated and shunned by all and scattered over the earth."

Brynych told his audience, simple Czech peasants, exactly what they already believed. He fit together skillfully the old maledictions the clergy had been pronouncing for centuries with the new anger experienced daily by the Czech masses: the Jews are cursed and shunned and subject to massacres in punishment for a dreadful ancient crime, the killing of Christ. "Let his blood be upon us and our sons," repeated Brynych at key points of his speech. The Jews were said to be "without altar or priests," cursed criminals but also godless, hence doubly dangerous. And to make matters worse, they were "a people without Fatherland or King," another striking characteristic of their shameless and exceptional condition. A cursed people, godless and nationless, they were the exact opposite of the Czech nation who were presented as God-fearing, obedient, and, above all, a people with a land of its own.

Lest anyone quarrel with his description of the cursed Jews, Brynych insisted that he was only stating historical truth, "what all eyes can see." Against the evidence of history and common sense, there was no recourse. "The truth cannot be suppressed by the Jews who dominate the press," nor can the Jews be saved from their deserved punishment just because "certain governments love them wholeheartedly and protect them."

This embrace of Czech grievances, of Czech hostility toward the government in Vienna and the liberal press, was grafted onto the Catholic Church's medieval propaganda triumph featuring accusations of ritual murder. Brynych dismissed those who might have had doubts about his claims. "You cannot confiscate the gospel" any more than you can deny a "historical fact." After all, the story of the most publicized child martyr of all time, Simon, the innocent little boy who was said to have been killed by the Jews in the city of Trent on March 25, 1472, "is not to be questioned." In fact, the story of Simon of Trent had recently been exhumed and published in the diocesan newsletter to provide a persuasive context for the Polná case. The ritual murder of little Simon can hardly be dismissed, Brynych told his listeners. As a result of the most searching investigation carried out by Church officials, there could be no doubt that this innocent child "was tied to the cross, his blood drained and collected for use in the making of unleavened bread. This awful event," thundered the bishop, "keeps alive the eternal outcry: His blood be upon us and our sons."

"Some gentlemen do not want to see this blood of which I speak," continued Brynych, intent upon confounding skeptics. Are they blind? Do they hate Catholics? They will not deprive us of the conviction deeply rooted in our hearts, the conviction that from each of those ritual murders "the blood itself calls out: His blood be upon us and our sons." "Someone might object: what curse is it that falls upon the Jews? Where is the evidence that they are a cursed people? Are they not in fact doing very well indeed? Are they not getting rich? Do they not lord it over all the Christians?" Neatly, the bishop went on to that other popular theme, the righteous indignation of ordinary folk who believe that the Jews exploit them. This rich vein of popular anger allowed the orator to speak to the hopes of his listeners while inviting mob violence. Why are the Jews doing so well if they are a cursed people? Well, asked the bishop, "could this very success, and the way they are lording it over us, at last force Christians to wake up?"

This suggestion, as he knew only too well, was by no means a new idea for his listeners. He followed it up with an open threat: "If the governments do not soon pull themselves together, if they cannot protect Christians, then something could happen, something that would be anything but a blessing." This nameless "something" reverberated in his listeners' minds. They knew the solution to the "Jewish problem." It was the same solution the Romans had opted for eighteen centuries earlier: "New blood, that must be our solution. New Christian blood."

At this point Brynych departed from rational methods of persuasion even further. His statements make no sense when read in cold blood, so to speak. But they made perfectly good sense to his audience. He was not conveying information, after all. He was not telling his listeners something they didn't know. He was merely providing moral sanction for their secret desires. He needed only to shout about blood, spilled Christian blood, drained from innocent children, and his audience would respond. "Christians are held in bondage," he shouted. "The Jews hold them in the bondage of the new paganism." The time had come to stop being accommodating, peaceful, and tolerant. Christians did not have to be accommodating to the point of "allowing their blood to be sucked out. What is needed," cried the bishop, "is new blood, and if this blood is allowed to irrigate the Austrian empire, we Czechs would soon enough get what we yearn for." There would be no need for a conflict with the Germans. "Innocent blood would not have been spilled, had our State been filled with this new blood. Let us work for the strengthening of Christendom in our Fatherland, so that clean blood may flow once again in our veins."

The message was that the removal of the Jews is the only possible solution to the difficulties experienced by dutiful Czech Catholics. To prevent further crimes against innocent Christian girls like Agnes Hruza, to liberate the Czech people from the oppression of Jewish capitalists and journalists, there was only one solution: to remove the infection, "so that clean blood may once again flow in our veins." And if public officials

48

refused to cooperate with the righteous avengers of innocent victims, "let them beware, lest the people take matters into their own hands."

Brynych reminded his listeners, as if they needed reminding, that things used to be under control not so long ago, when the Jews were kept in their place, when they were not allowed to mingle with Christians. It was only in recent years that a heathen liberal state had given the Jews free rein to exploit, to dominate, to murder Christians. This must end, he demanded, by legal means, if possible or, failing that, the Jews would fare much worse.

What was the threat here? How was the cleansing to be carried out? Just what practical measures could be contemplated in the search for a solution to the "Jewish problem?" It was always at this point that professional antisemites fell short of providing a plausible answer. What was to be done? Could you turn back, in the early years of the twentieth century, to the restrictive laws of an earlier time? Could you reinvent the ghetto? Could you drive the Jews out of Czech lands? Would the Jews offer resistance? Could you abolish their rights by edict? Confiscate their property, destroy their temples, as had been done in the past? Was this feasible, without undermining the economy?

Bishop Brynych and his followers were not statesmen or policy makers. They tended not to worry too much about what was feasible. Instead, they tried to win favor with the masses. They worked to sabotage the functioning of the constitutional state. In the Austrian parliament, which was becoming a caricature of a parliamentary system, there was no need to present practical measures. "The Jews' heads are swelling, they are starting to act real impudent," said one deputy on May 13, 1899, when the Polná case was on everyone's mind. "The Jews should be driven out," shouted another. Even more eloquently, Deputy Scheicher, a Catholic priest, declared that "the times in which we live remind me of that period in which the German people suffered its deepest humiliation under Napoleon. The time has come to stop sparing the Jews. They must no longer be allowed to build their houses on Christian soil. No Jew should be permitted to set foot in a university. Let us do away with the synagogues. From now on we must wage a war of annihilation against the Jews." His remarks were met with stormy applause from the audience.

Wild statements of this kind were becoming common. They were reported daily in respectable papers and cheered in the gutter press. The sheer force of repetition and the fact that those provocations were not challenged contributed to a passive acceptance of vicious fantasies. Hardly anyone was now in the position to defend the liberal policies in public. The occasional deputy who, shocked by the coarse bullying that was now the daily fare of Austrian politics, stood up in protest was soon shouted down by the likes of Gregorig, Wolff, Scheicher, Iro, or Turk. When a rare Jewish member of the Viennese city council stood up to speak, he was attacked by the Christian Socialist majority. Dr. Stern, for instance, invoked his right to speak and insisted on his patriotic credentials. "I am a good Austrian and a good Viennese," he said.

"*Dank schön*," crowed one of his tormentors in broad Viennese dialect. "*Sie san ja a Jud und ka Wiener*" (Sure, sure, let's face it, you're a Jew, not a Viennese). When Dr. Sontag, a Social Democrat, moved up to the podium, he was greeted with cries of "*Judenknecht*" (servant of Jews). The shouting that day in the city council, March 16, 1899, concerned a debate over the extension of voting rights to a broader category of Viennese inhabitants, a popular proposal. "Everyone in Austria should have the right to vote, except the Jews" was the succinct summary of one speaker's position.

A few weeks later, after the Polná case had surfaced, the talk in the Austrian parliament became truly wild. The rare speaker who refused to join the rowdy tide was shouted down with cries of "*Echt Jüdisch*" and "*So ein Judendiener.*" Or "*Er ist ein Jud und kein Mensch*" (he is a Jew, not a human being). The same deputy, Gregorig, who had denied in March that a Jew could be a patriot and a citizen, now denied that a Jew could be a human being at all. No topic remained neutral in the course of those debates. Lueger, the semi-respectable mayor of Vienna, kept in the swim by thundering against the presence of Jews in the medical profession. Lueger, who was the most powerful politician in Austria, gave Gregorig and company credibility by embracing their gutter rhetoric. The mayor's favorite word appeared to be "*verjudung*" (Jewification). He spoke of the "*verjudung*" of the medical school and stressed the importance of having "German Christian doctors." Entire professions were denounced as "*verjudet,*" as were entire cities such as Linz, Hitler's hometown.

Words like *verjudung* were designed to heap contempt, in the most vulgar and brutal way, on the targets of the politicians' ire. The words imply infestation, contagion, exposure to vermin. Even Social Democrats, like the Polish deputy Daszyński, who personally had no animus against Jews, found themselves playing to the gallery as the parliament was increasingly turned into a circus. While making a point about the disintegration of national unity in the empire, Daszyński grabbed the chamber's attention by mentioning the Jews: "Even the Jews," he said, "are looking for a national homeland." This was the most extreme example of separatism he could think of. "Yes," he added, "the crassest example: even the Jews are gravitating towards Palestine." Why was this the crassest example? No matter. To use the word *Jude*, to mention Jews in an inevitably contemptuous context, played well with the audience.

Daszyński did not go far enough for his audience, however. It was expected that when you mentioned Jews, you also had to mention their departure. A voice shouted out, after his remark about the Jews thinking of Palestine, "*Nur fort mit Ihnen*" (away with them). The lengths to which loose talk about getting rid of their Jewish neighbors could reach was illustrated by Gregorig's response, in the course of a discussion of rural electrification on May 19, 1899. Gregorig appeared to favor the extension of electric power lines. An opponent asked what good they are. "Good?" replied Gregorig. "I'll tell you what they are good for. They are good for hanging Jews."

What conclusions did Austrian Jews draw from the constant barrage of threats? There were several possible reactions, the most common of which was simply to ignore the tumult and the shouting while keeping a low profile and going on with one's business. Pushing this strategy to its logical conclusion, some chose to ignore their own Jewishness. Others fled in the opposite direction, giving up on assimilation, having reached the conclusion that they would always remain strangers in a hostile land no matter what they did. Many chose emigration, especially to America.

No breach had as yet been made in the legal situation of Austrian Jews. On paper, in the eyes of the law, they continued to enjoy all the guarantees devised since 1848. In spite of the threats, the accusations, the riots and the boycotts, the liberal laws still stood in 1914, as frail as the empire itself, frailer than most people imagined. And all the while

Jews continued to fill the classrooms of the most selective schools, crowded into university lecture halls and laboratories, published books and newspapers, wrote plays and symphonies and managed factories, and appeared to dominate the medical and legal professions—in short, they seemed to be on top everywhere except in politics. This profound discrepancy between the actual place Jews occupied and the place to which most Christians wished to relegate them built to an almost unbearable tension.

CHAPTER~THREE

BIELITZ WAS A SMALL, PROSPEROUS, INDUSTRIAL TOWN, German-speaking and, almost uniquely in the empire, part Protestant and part Jewish. It may have been spared some of the tensions familiar to the residents of Vienna and many Czech cities. Hugo grew up in a safe, uneventful little world, protected from the fissures that appeared elsewhere. His own experience hardly reflected the antisemitic excesses reported in the daily press. The closest he came, it seems, to feeling the turbulence of those days, on the eve of the catastrophe of 1914, was on that roof when he decided that the girl's talk of the "white race" was poisonous.

The overwhelming impression the reader of Hugo Huppert's memoirs comes away with is that the author's childhood was a safe foundation for a life that would turn out to be far from safe. Hugo, writing from the perspective of a man who had experienced exile, war, prison, and, above all, the loss of his dearest, *"meine liebsten,"* looked back on those prewar years as a childhood paradise permanently suffused with sunshine and peace. "Each day of the week came through the doors of our home as a friend: it was peacetime," he wrote. Before 1914, in peacetime Bielitz-Biala, a young boy like Hugo could thrive in the warm embrace of his family and his neighborhood.

As he looked back on those happy years, the elderly poet was home again in his imagination. He began writing his memoirs on a windy spring morning in Vienna in 1974, assisted by a young archivist, Sigrid Anger, who had come from Communist East Berlin to make an inventory of Hugo's surviving papers, on deposit at the Akademie der Künste. Digging through the archive, Fräulein Anger found an astonishing artifact: Hugo's original birth certificate. Astonishing, because survivors like Hugo very rarely have access to physical remains of their past.

The document was signed by Rabbi Markus Glaser. It gives the town of Lipnik as Hugo's birthplace. But wait, said Hugo, taking a close look at the birth certificate: there is a mistake here! Yes, I was born on Thursday, June 5, 1902, in my parents' apartment, at number 9, Alznerstrasse, but not in Lipnik: in Biala! The Alznerstrasse, leading past the Jewish cemetery to the German-speaking village of Alzen, was the dividing line between Lipnik and Biala. The right side was in Lipnik, the left in Biala. And number 9 was on the left side. Therefore Hugo was born in Biala.

Is this pointless pedantry? I do not think so. Wherever he went, wherever he lived, Hugo was in the habit of providing the exact address and accurate directions, telling the reader how to get to his destination, even if the destination no longer existed, even if it vanished long ago, together with the men, women, and children who once lived there. I cannot help thinking that Hugo's painstaking reconstruction of a lifetime of obsolete addresses is a way of securing the past that survives only in words.

The Alznerstrasse may still run between Biala and Lipnik, even the three-story apartment house at number 9 could quite possibly still be standing, but the people he knew and loved before 1939 are sure to have vanished. That alone acts as a powerful incentive for recording what can be salvaged from those "islands of memory"—Hugo's expression—set in the vast emptiness created by two savage wars. The salvage operation begun that spring in 1974 was made possible by Hugo's lifelong attention to observing and recording the world around him.

He started recording his experiences at an early age, preparing to become a writer. He tells us that he learned to use shorthand notation, following the Gabelsberger method, by the time he was ten or eleven. He acquired the habit of transcribing his notes into ordinary notebooks of the kind used in schools. Some of those notebooks found their permanent resting place in the archives of the Berlin Akademie der Künste, where I was able to consult them recently. Hugo's habit of recording what he saw, what he heard, what he thought about, would allow him, many years later, to recapture key experiences of those early years. Some of those memories, presented now as finished, expertly told stories, almost certainly are genuine, even if they are not exact accounts of what happened.

As someone whose understanding of psychology was influenced by ideas floating around in the Vienna of the 1920s, Freud's Vienna and Schnitzler's, Hugo was on the lookout for early manifestations of desire. He never forgot the servant girl, pretty young Susi, whose caresses at bedtime, when little Hugo would have been about four years old, were entirely different from his mother's embraces. On some evenings Susi would let her long, blond hair down as she leaned over the boy, covering his face and provoking shudders of delight.

And then there was Kasia, a Polish peasant woman in her thirties, who gave the boy his evening bath. Wearing only a long nightgown, which became wet as the boy splashed in his bath, Kasia let her nightgown drop to the floor. Hugo, now age six, is overcome with strange emotions. He hurls his wet and soapy body against Kasia's naked thighs. She holds him tight and groans. The scene is regularly reenacted, with the bathroom door locked.

From an early age, Hugo would find himself in thrall to girls, unable to resist their blandishments. As a four-year-old, he was in love with his next door neighbor, Hede Auspitz, whom he remembered in later years as the little girl with the upswept blond hair tied with a broad sky-blue bow. When he entered kindergarten, Hugo enjoyed playing with the girls in "Aunt Lina's" kindergarten class. The elderly writer still remembered how the teacher appeared to the four-year-old boy: a tall, powerful woman in her fifties, her gray hair swept up in carefully controlled braids, a suggestion of a mustache, and the scent of a perfumed soap. Judging from his surviving notebooks, filled with the near-calligraphy of his observations, Hugo Huppert developed an ability for observing the world in close-up from an early age. His portraits of the children he knew and of the adults important to him, sketched quickly, with the professional writer's sure touch, bring his childhood universe to life.

The power of memory is the animating spirit of Hugo's voluminous memoirs, nowhere more evocative than in his recreation of his Bielitz childhood. You can actually smell the lost world of his past. Again and again, he is reminded of significant scents: the teacher's soap, the smell of the colorful clay the children handled, the powerful scent of the turpentine used at home to scrub floors clean. The aroma of turpentine, reminiscent of the pine forests of his childhood, was the scent of home for him. He confessed that he had been in the habit of carrying a pocket-sized perfume bottle filled with a distilled version of that hometown elixir all those years when he was away in Vienna during his student days, and in exile, in Russia, in later years.

In his memoirs Hugo gives free rein to his passion for meticulous evocations of people and settings, especially those anchored in his imagination when he remembers his Bielitz childhood. He was comfortably ensconced in the warm nest of his parental home. At the center of this warm nest was his mother, Anna, whom he remembered as the benign source of all good things. Although he very rarely, if at all, refers to his mother, this being too painful for him, he does, eventually, in the last year of his life, draw a quick portrait of her. He sees her walking in rainy weather, taking quick steps, with only one thing on her mind: were her boys out in the rain, getting soaked? In a calmer setting, he sees her playing the zither, with her eyes closed. She also painted landscapes she had never actually seen. "Mother taught me to look at life hopefully, without fear," wrote the old poet.

Hugo was growing up under his mother's tutelage while his father was climbing the ladder of success in the Austrian Imperial civil service. He would come home for lunch, say very little, take a twenty-minute nap under cover of his newspaper, and return to his post office. It was Anna who talked with the boy, sang to him, played the piano for him, and introduced the child to the worthwhile pleasures of life. In summer, she would take Hugo, and, eventually, his younger brother, Josef, to her ancestral home, set amid orchards in their home village where Abraham Huppert first met Anna.

Around 1905, the family moved from the peripheral Alznerstrasse to the more centrally located Franzensplatz, a wide, inviting square where the young boys ran wild and kicked improvised footballs around, directly in front of Feiner's grocery store. The Huppert family rented an apartment on the fourth floor of this solid new building owned by David Feiner. Across from Feiner's store one found Kehler's pharmacy and Gisitzky's bookstore, where German-language books were displayed next to Polish-language ones. The easy coexistence of German and Polish was the hallmark of the local culture. At home, too, while Hugo's mother was fluent in Polish and spoke it with the servants, Father Huppert spoke only German with Hugo.

It was not quite a bilingual world. The parents spoke German to each other and to Hugo. The maids, Susi and soon Kasia too, spoke Polish, or, to be more precise, the local Silesian Polish with German words mixed in. This was called "*po naszemu*," meaning "our way." The shopkeepers in the neighborhood tended to be German-speaking, Jewish men of a background similar to Adolf Huppert's. In the summer, when Anna took Hugo with her to the Reich family compound, they were among both Polish and German-speakers.

The kindergarten, a public institution located in the complex of school buildings at the end of the Tuchmachergasse, was German-speaking, and so were, almost without exception, the members of the Hupperts' social world. Hugo was still too young to have anything to do with the Reform temple his parents attended on the High Holy Days. With few exceptions, his tight little world was at first limited to the Franzensplatz and to Tante Lina's class.

One of these exceptions was the occasional visit with the elderly Krauss sisters, Dory and Tilly. They were twins and had never married. Very musical, the sisters were in the habit of playing piano for four hands on their old Bösendorfer instrument: Mozart overtures or Schumann pieces. The very first accords produced an astounding transformation in the child, according to his mother's testimony in later years: eyes wide open, mouth open, the boy would freeze on the spot, overcome with awe. Music was to play an important role in Hugo's life.

In the classroom and at home, he was surrounded by girls, by women. Between Anna, Susi, Kasia, and Hede, the neighbors' child, little Hugo could give in to his natural attraction to those mysterious and benign creatures, to their soft bodies and enticing aromas. It was his mother, to be sure, whom he worshipped above all. She taught the boy to sing, to draw, to acquire language at breakneck speed. In later years she would arrange for piano lessons and have an upright piano delivered to their home. It was Anna, too, who took the boy to local musical events.

Anna Huppert painted watercolors and played the zither. She was deeply attached to her parental home, the village tavern, with its apple orchard and duck pond. Even after her father's death, she was in the habit of spending a good deal of time in the summer months with her brothers' families at the old homestead. The Reich family owned farms, even a sizeable estate. One of the Reich brothers managed a hotel in Kraków, another was away in the Ukraine, in charge of railway construction. As for Anna's sister, Flora, she had married Maurice Beck, a successful jewelry manufacturer in Paris.

Clearly, the Reichs were entirely different from the Hupperts of Bochnia, about whom Hugo knew nothing. There were no photographs of his Huppert grandparents and his father never spoke of them. It was only much later, as an adult, when Hugo spent a year in Paris, that he met his uncle Emmanuel, his father's brother, who lived there, in the Jewish quarter of the Marais neighborhood. Emmanuel, like his brother Abraham, had left home many years earlier. He learned a trade in Germany, working with furs and pelts. His was a quiet, modest, traditional life. He still spoke Yiddish, staying with his wife, Paula, among other Galician Jews who had re-created the shtetls of their childhood, right in the center of the French capital, rue de la Grange Batellière.

Back in Bielitz, the family's fortunes kept rising. With help from Anna's sister Flora and her wealthy husband, the Bielitz Hupperts joined the local frenzy for capital investment. They ordered the construction of a sizeable apartment building that would house eight apartments, including the one to be occupied by the Huppert family. Situated at 6 Tuchmachergasse, the new apartment became Hugo's cherished family home from the time of his ninth birthday. Soon after, the boy began to attend school in Bielitz, where he eventually entered the Gymnasium, from which he would graduate in 1920.

Those formative years in Bielitz are lovingly evoked in the first volume of Hugo's memoirs. Aside from the stringent requirements of the classroom, Hugo, like most German-speaking boys his age, fell head over heels into the imaginary world of Karl May's novels featuring the German adventurer Old Shatterhand and his friend, the Indian Chief Winnetou, as they proceeded into the American Wild West. Books, music, and close friendships with other boys at the Gymnasium propelled Hugo into a feverish intellectual life under the guidance of Otto Schneid, who was two years ahead of him at school.

Schneid was the talented and charismatic leader of their group. He was a poet and an artist who kept up with the latest cultural developments in Vienna and beyond. The *Neue Freie Presse* provided daily reports on Viennese literary, musical, and political events and debates. Soon, Hugo, following in Otto's wake, became a passionate admirer of the reigning provocateur on Vienna's literary scene, Karl Kraus, whose publication, *Die Fackel*, in its red cover, was eagerly awaited by the Bielitz faction of Kraus followers. "We believed in Karl Kraus, and Otto was his prophet," writes Hugo, so many years later, tongue in cheek. Otto Schneid became a well-known artist and art historian. When things became truly dangerous in Vienna, Otto found refuge in Palestine and, later, in Toronto. He got in touch with Hugo when it became possible, and he had the distinction of being one of the very rare friends from Bielitz who were still alive when Hugo sat down to write his memoirs.

Back in their student days, Otto's leadership was indisputable. His girlfriend, Olga Langer, lived with her family in one of the Huppert apartments at 6 Tuchmachergasse. She had access to the newest and most arcane literature, books not available in the local book stores. From her book shelves, volume after volume would find its way to Hugo and other members of Otto's circle, each book carrying the scent of Olga's perfume. Strindberg, Rilke, Werfel, Georg Trakl, Martin Buber, Hermann Hesse, and the young Johannes R. Becher were to be found among Olga's treasures, as well as Chinese poetry and the output of the avant-garde publishing houses, including Rowohlt and Insel. Karl Kraus's *Fackel*, in its aggressive cover, was devoured as soon as it reached the Langers' mailbox.

Hugo recalls his school years in astonishing detail, making it clear that the Bielitz Gymnasium had served as the foundation of his intellectual life. His portraits of his teachers are sharply drawn, thanks to his astonishing memory and, no doubt, to his lifelong journal keeping. The gallery of outstanding teachers includes Dr. Julius Werner, who was "like a father" to Hugo. Next to Dr. Werner there was Karl Haar, who initiated the boy into the intricacies of prosody, lent him books, and invited him to his home. Then there was Emil Wetschera, an elegant man who wrote plays and taught history and geography. For science, Hugo remembers Dr. Hans Krawany, whose appearance came close to being grotesque. His large head, resting on a short body, could easily have invited scorn, but the man was respected and beloved, his teaching of science masterful. Dr. Krawany was a materialist who rejected faith and embraced reason. Among elective studies, Hugo chose French and stenography, both subjects eminently practical, since he was already acquainted with the Gabelsberger shorthand method and since his French relatives in Paris, Uncle Emmanuel and Aunt Flora, were in correspondence with his parents.

Between the intoxicating literary excursions in Otto's wake, the demanding schoolwork at the Gymnasium, and the opening to the world, especially in the war years, one might conclude that these young people were focused exclusively on literature, music, and politics. Bielitz, however, had other treasures on offer, especially the mountains and forests visible from Hugo's bedroom window. Led by Otto, the group hiked in the woods, starting out in the Zigeunerwald—the Gypsy Woods— an expansive parkland only three kilometers from downtown, easily reached by electric streetcar. Hugo maintained a special, soothing relationship with those woods. Unlucky in love, rejected by a girl, he found solace in the Zigeunerwald.

He was not alone to seek comfort there. A particularly dramatic episode he recalls provides an opportunity for deploying his storytelling talent. This involved the suicide of a friend, Isi Körber, a boy a year younger whose sister, Lilli, was part of Otto's group. Hugo would have been seventeen at the time. The year was 1919.

The story begins with a phone call from Otto. "Drop everything and come quickly," said Otto. "This is about the life or death of a friend! You know Isi Körber. He has been missing since yesterday. His parents are desperate, they reported him missing. Isi's sister, Lilli, heard him say some things that make her fear the worst. If he is trying to kill himself, he most likely is headed for the Zigeunerwald. We have to look for him there. Come, I don't know anyone else who could help me now."

They boarded the streetcar. At the edge of the woods, which were covered with a thin dusting of new snow, there were no tracks. This was a weekday, and no one was there. The tree trunks were white on their northern side. All at once, Otto cried out: "Here, here, come quickly." Hugo threw himself against the underbrush, almost losing his balance, calling out to Otto as the frightened crows took off, scattering snow from the highest branches. And there was Otto, standing motionless over Isi's lifeless body at the entrance to the well-known shelter called the Stefansruhe.

They kneeled next to the frozen body, reading the note Isi left and taking in the litter of empty morphine vials. They cried. Then they made a decision: Otto would run off to get help, Hugo would stay with the body. Darkness descended. At last Otto returned, accompanied by a village policeman in uniform. At this point Nathan Gloffner, Isi's best friend, joined them and began to cry. Otto then ran off again into the night, having failed to reach the Körber family earlier. The village gendarme came around and pulled a lantern out of his backpack, sitting down on a log and muttering, in broken Polish: "Poor boy, kills himself for no reason. *Och, biedny chłopiec, biedny chłopiec.*" Danilo, the old gendarme, began to hum sad Ukrainian melodies under his mustache. Hugo is deeply affected by all this.

At seventeen, he was a practiced note taker, using shorthand to write down what people were saying. Soon he would be in Vienna, listening to customers in local bars, noting their stories, their way of expressing things, their words. The suicide of Isi was one kind of story. Hugo's first sexual experience made for another kind. In this instance Hugo was fourteen. He persuaded an older boy, Anton Czapka, to take him along to the local brothel.

Arriving in front of the notorious house down by the river, they knocked on the solid wooden door and were allowed in, past heavy red drapes. The matron, wearing a lavender silk kimono, was heavily perfumed. She greeted Anton and joked about the new customer he had brought with him: "We don't want to open a kindergarten here, now do we?" She did not seem to want to allow Hugo to stay but gave in to the boys' pleas, so long as Anton assumed full responsibility. Soon enough, the woman launched into her practiced sales pitch: "For you I have here a very special bird of paradise, a terrific creature, not much older than you are, I think. She is from Croatia, from a corn-growing village near Gottschee, ever heard of that town? That's where we get the prettiest girls in the world."

The madam turned to the stairs. "Draga, Draga, come down, you are wanted!" she called out, keeping up a soothing patter, while young Hugo, spellbound and mute, invoked the Roman poet Ovidius Naso, who knew what to say in such circumstances. And then, pretty Draga arrived, holding out her hand and smiling at the underage customer. She was wearing a saffron-colored wrap over a geranium-red tunic and ivory-colored Turkish-style trousers. She had green eyes. The boys can't take their own eyes off her.

"My name is Draga," she said to Hugo. "Why are you laughing?" Hugo is probably laughing because he is embarrassed. "How old are you anyway? Are you experienced? I mean, with girls and such?" The boy climbed the stairs to the girl's attic room, fearful at first. He recalled a scene from Boccaccio's *Decameron*, noted the perfume Draga was wearing, watched her as she started taking off her clothes. "Would you want me to keep my stockings on?" she asked. Hugo, now more at ease, rolled down her stockings, and as he became involved in this task he suddenly thought of Susi, the pretty young woman who took care of him when he was four years old. He imagined Susi looking like Draga when she was getting ready for bed or about to take a bath.

That evening experience with Draga is brought to life by the elderly writer. Was the fourteen-year-old boy already able to mimic the speech of prostitutes and madams? Most likely, considering the emotional impact of that evening, he would have written down his impressions at the time. But the version of the event presented in his memoir is sure to have been improved by the old poet looking back on his childhood. His method is what he calls "poetic reportage."

It was the common way in which talented writers reported on events and persons in the feuilleton pages of Viennese newspapers. "Feuilleton," in its original French sense, referred to the serialized publication of novels in daily papers. In German-language newspapers the word acquired a different meaning: a new kind of writing, more personal and subjective. In the feuilleton section of German and Austrian papers, one could read stories of the kind that Hugo wrote, stories like that of Isi's suicide in the Zigeunerwald. At one time Theodor Herzl, the founder of Zionism, had been the feuilleton editor of the *Neue Freie*. Perhaps the all-time champion of this kind of personal reporting with a difference was Egon Erwin Kisch, whom Hugo admired and whose mentoring he sought. Kisch, originally from Prague, was another Jewish Communist writer at home everywhere and always on the go. He spent the difficult years in Mexico, among other places, not in Russia. After the war, Hugo visited him in Prague and edited a collection of his stories.

By the time of his encounter with Draga, Hugo was no longer a child. At fourteen, he was a precocious young man, moving through the classes of the Bielitz Gymnasium and fully involved with his literary and musical friends, Otto's gang. He was also becoming knowledgeable about the world beyond his hometown. He is old enough now to spend time in the big city, Kraków, where Anna's relatives opened their homes to the boy and where he discovered opera. Standing in line to buy cheap tickets, he soon found his way to the glittering evening performances of *Carmen, Madama Butterfly,* and *Faust.* From his perch in the gallery, he could look down on the audience in the orchestra seats where beautiful women in all their finery fascinated the boy. Their perfumes made their way up to the galleries.

Looking at Hugo, so comfortable at home, among his friends, in the classrooms of his fine school, in the familiar city with its horizon of woods and mountains, how could anyone foresee a future as a hunted exile far removed from everything that had mattered to him as he left home at the age of eighteen? In his old age, Hugo rarely slipped into nostalgic evocations of that peacetime paradise, his beloved Bielitz. On occasion, though, and obliquely, his sense of loss is crystallized in the words of a simple poem, as in the case of "Dorf Alzen," a bitter remembrance of the village of Alzen, at the end of the Alznerstrasse. This poem, like the one recalling his mother in the rain, is a very late one, published in the last year of his life.

It is a simple poem. The poet remembers the farmer from Alzen who used to deliver asparagus, onions, and milk, never raising his whip as his horses trotted along, knowing the way. We read about the butter from Alzen, and the honey and the flowers. *In Alzen herrscht Frieden,* peace reigns in Alzen. And where are the people of Alzen today? The war destroyed the land. Where are the farmers now? The ruined farmsteads are blackened. The pleasures of peacetime, when the farmers brought all that was needed to the households of Bielitz, those sumptuous pleasures, long gone, are remembered in awe and, belatedly, acknowledged with thanks.

War was on the horizon, that summer of 1914. Russia was very close, although Kraków and Bielitz were never attacked. But the war gradually changed everything. Wounded soldiers evacuated from the front lines were housed in local schools. Food was becoming scarce. And by the time of the armistice of November 1918, the world had been drastically transformed. The old empire was dead. Bielitz was no longer in Austria. It was now part of the new Polish Republic.

Hugo and his classmates were still able to graduate from the German-language Gymnasium, but the institution would soon become Polish. Street names were changed. Adolf Huppert still kept his position at the post office, but in many ways the old order was broken. This became particularly obvious when Hugo, having graduated, left Bielitz in 1920 to become a student at the university in Vienna. His father accompanied him, making the transition easier for the eighteen-year-old. But once they boarded the train, the venerable Nordbahn, there was no hiding the effect of the convulsions of the last four years.

In the course of what turned out to be a forty-two-hour voyage, the fissures the war years had opened became visible: what had once been a smooth journey had been turned into a nightmare. The third-class compartments, overcrowded to bursting, had lost their windows. The train stopped at four separate border controls where the passengers were ordered to carry their suitcases into the customs offices; there they were searched, in turn, by Czech, Polish, and Austrian officials. Where there had once been a vast empire within which you could travel without papers, there were now separate nations with different languages and uniforms, all at odds with each other. Hugo saw all this as a return to the time of the Thirty Years' War.

In the train compartment there was only a single survivor from peacetime: Hugo's capacious leather suitcase, made to order by a local tanner in Bielitz. That suitcase would house Hugo's belongings for years to come, as he carried it across borders, to Paris, to Moscow, to the Soviet Far East.

CHAPTER—FOUR

THE SORRY STATE OF RAILWAY TRAVEL ACROSS THE DIVIDED remains of the old empire was symptomatic of far more ominous breakdowns. In his hurry to begin life as an independent adult in the big city, Hugo may have ignored the profound dislocations in the new Polish Republic and in the other regions abandoned by the defeated empire: Communist revolution in Hungary, major uprisings elsewhere, the new Soviet state at war against Polish troops, and, everywhere, attacks against the Jewish population, even in quiet Teschen, next door to Bielitz—now Bielsko.

In Polish cities, including Kraków, Lwów, and Lublin, riots and pogroms directed against the local Jewish population were frequent in 1918 and 1919. The Polish Catholic clergy fanned the flames. The right-wing press was vociferous in its denunciations of Jews. Meanwhile, inflation was rising to absurd levels: the Polish mark sat at 160 against the dollar as Hugo headed for Vienna. A year later, it would be at 45,000 and by 1923 at 140,000.

The Huppert family could hardly have been oblivious to the savage attacks against local Jewish families, which began almost immediately after the collapse of the Austrian monarchy, in November 1918. A report published in the *Times* of London on Saturday, February 8, 1919, mentioned pogroms in 110 different localities. In all of them, shops were plundered, houses were looted, Jews were brutally assaulted. The rioters were generally peasants from neighboring villages. Particular savagery was displayed at Komarówka, near Biala. There, Polish soldiers—that is to say, Polish peasants armed and in uniform—seized Jewish men and beat them with whips and rods, all the while extracting money from the victims.

After years of senseless killing in the trenches, authority vanished in Germany, Poland, Hungary, and Russia. In the absence of effective government, insurgencies of various sorts erupted. The Hungarian Soviet experiment under Béla Kun quickly collapsed, replaced by proto-fascist armed groups. In Germany, such groups were murderous, as were their Polish equivalents. In Russia the Bolsheviks took over, while in Italy Mussolini's thugs took a little longer to conquer power. The twentieth century was beginning to acquire its distinctive hue. Spain was lagging behind, joining the fray in the 1930s, by which time Germany had come under the malignant rule of Adolf Schicklgruber, also called Hitler, an Austrian war veteran who managed to express the wild frustrations of an entire generation shaped by war, defeat, and destitution.

Vienna, Red Vienna, where Hugo landed in the early fall of 1920, was different. The huge metropolis of a vanished empire, some two million strong, had become the capital city of a new, small republic. Equipped with a new constitution drafted by Hans Kelsen, a young professor at the university, Vienna held municipal elections that brought the Social Democrats to power, backed by the city's labor unions. The new administration adopted progressive policies, especially in dealing with the extreme housing shortage. Ambitious apartment complexes were built, in spite of postwar shortages and financial difficulties.

There was poverty and overcrowding, inflation and hunger, in part caused by the constant influx of displaced people fleeing the pervasive violence in the eastern lands of the erstwhile empire. Yet, with all that, Vienna was welcoming. Not only to students from the provinces, such as Hugo and his friends, but to political refugees. Active revolutionaries, displaced and hunted by their opponents, set up shop here, publishing newspapers and tracts. Victor Serge was there, editing the Comintern newspaper. Antonio Gramsci was there, and so was the Comintern's Georgi Dimitroff. One could attend lectures by the French pacifist writer Henri Barbusse or play chess with Leon Trotsky.

The years that corresponded to Hugo's university studies were marked by the policies of Otto Bauer's Social Democrats. Vienna's mayor, Jakob Reumann, led the reforms that were to create large numbers of affordable housing units and healthcare for the poor. Hugo's own experiences with dreadful housing options fill a number of pages in his memoirs. He moved from one hopeless sublet to another. Fortunately, he was able to return home during the long summer vacations. Home meant everything to him, his mother above all, but also his father, who clearly cared for the boy without being blind to his more obvious shortcomings. After months of genuine privation, including a five-week stay in a hospital for a lung infection, Hugo's return to Bielitz in the summer months meant plentiful food and fresh air.

Vienna, to be sure, was exciting. In spite of being desperately lonely at times, Hugo quickly came to love the city. It had so much to offer and there was so much to learn there. There were Karl Kraus's lectures and readings, where Hugo met up with his Bielitz friends and fellow Kraus worshippers, Otto, Leo, and Erwin. Thanks to another of his Bielitz friends, Erich Werner, a talented musician, Hugo found himself included among the invited guests to weekly meetings of the Friends of Arnold Schönberg. These were concert performances of new music by Schönberg, Alban Berg, Anton von Webern, and others in their circle. They met in the conference room of the Schwarzwald School.

This private school for gifted girls run by Genia Schwarzwald was another avant-garde institution, on par with the musical meetings of the Friends of Arnold Schönberg. The school's graduates tended to be high-strung, often Jewish, girls with limitless ambition and left-wing sympathies, among them, for instance, Rosa Stern, who under her own chosen name of Lucie, and her married name, Varga, would become a medievalist and the collaborator of Lucien Febvre, of the Collège de France. Her articles would appear in the 1930s in Febvre's journal, the famous *Annales*. They were groundbreaking studies of fascism. Lucie was an unstoppable risk taker, climbing Alpine ridges and taking innocent-seeming train trips into Nazi Germany to collect information. She was at the time married to Franz Borkenau, a Marxist historian who was a leader in the Communist international youth movement until 1929, when he broke with Stalin and went on to become one of the most incisive critics of the Soviet system. Hugo, who was in Moscow by then, naturally goes on record in his memoirs to denounce Borkenau.

Among other extraordinary graduates of Genia Schwarzwald's school, there was Lou Eisler, the wife of the well-known composer Hanns Eisler. Lou had been married and divorced by the age of nineteen. She was a friend of Egon Erwin Kisch, became a Communist, and married Eisler. Eisler, a close friend of Bertolt Brecht, found refuge in the United States together with Lou, but was forced to return to Europe after the war because of his politics. Lou's next husband was the Austrian Communist journalist and political leader Ernst Fischer, who had spent the war years in Soviet exile while he was married to Ruth von Mayenburg. Hugo knew them both well.

To follow the intricate mix of marriages, divorces, love affairs, and political commitments characteristic of those years, when the old order was collapsing, is to enter into the intimate reality of a moment in history when everything hung in the balance, when new ideas, new music, new art and architecture, and new political programs kept the world in suspense. In a word: they were revolutionary times.

Hugo Huppert, wide-eyed in Red Vienna at eighteen, certainly sensed the break with the past as he followed his friends into theaters and literary cafés, relishing the energy emanating from all that was new. In his second year at the university, he participated in the seminars of Karl Grünberg and Hans Kelsen. Kelsen, a constitutional scholar whose draft of the Austrian Republic's constitution was the founding document of the new state, was popular with students. Hugo was in the habit of attending Professor Kelsen's Wednesday afternoon informal gatherings at his apartment (Wickenburgstrasse, corner Alserstrasse). Kelsen's young wife, a Schwarzwald graduate, and her little girls were there, too.

It sounds cozy and welcoming, but the darker side of Viennese student life was just then beginning to be noticed. Soon, right-wing students would be pushing their way into Professor Grünberg's lectures, screaming imprecations against "Jews and Marxists." At the main entrance to the university, crowds of men wearing swastikas pinned to their collars would be holding up placards with slogans such as "No dogs, Jews and Marxists allowed." These provocations would soon increase in frequency, especially after Mussolini's "March on Rome" on October 28, 1922. Professor Grünberg would leave Vienna for Frankfurt. Borkenau would join him there. Kelsen, who would soon feel threatened as well, would eventually end up at the University of California at Berkeley.

It was against this background that Hugo considered joining Kostufra, the Communist student group, and the KPÖ, the Austrian Communist Party. Among Kostufra's members there were young men who would become Hugo's lifelong friends, especially Helmut Liebknecht, the son of Karl Liebknecht, the murdered co-founder of the German Communist Party, and Vladimir Turok, a Bosnian student who would become a highly regarded historian of Austria. Hugo's decision, at the age of nineteen, to become a Communist was surprising, especially to his family, who did not approve. Years later Hugo was still trying to explain his motivation.

His old friends from Bielitz were less likely to become engaged in politics: Otto studied art history, Erwin chose chemistry, Erich pursued a career in music. Only one other Bielitz boy in Vienna, Harald Langer, joined the newly founded Austrian Communist Party. Neither Harald nor his sister, Olga, became students at the university. They became militant activists. Together with Paul Finder, who had grown up in Biala, they would meet regularly, stapling brochures and discussing politics. Guided by Dr. Johannes Wertheim of the radical publishing house Verlag für Literatur und Politik, Finder's group, which included Hugo, read their way through standard Marxist works and newly translated Russian books. Gradually, in Hugo's universe, Karl Kraus was being pushed aside by Karl Marx. Paul Finder eventually left for Moscow and, after the German invasion of Poland, became a heroic figure, playing a key role in the Polish Resistance under the name of Comrade Pawel. He was eventually captured by the Gestapo and murdered.

Hugo, who joined the KPÖ at the age of nineteen, may have been swayed by Finder's arguments and those of his new friends in the Kostufra group, but in the end it was the influence of a seventeen-year-old girl that was decisive. He noticed her from the streetcar on his way to a lecture and, soon after, he saw her again, walking along the Nussdor-ferstrasse. He persuaded her to let him accompany her. She was on her way to a meeting of the Austrian Proletarian Youth. Hugo explained that he was a Communist, a Party member. The girl, whose name was Emily Artbauer, agreed to let Hugo come along. The following Saturday evening he accompanied her to a meeting of her teenage study group.

Emily was obviously a leader. The boys and girls she led were suspicious of Hugo, to begin with, but clearly devoted to Emily. Hugo found himself deeply affected by what he described as "the aura of certainty" that emanated from the girl. He found it irresistible and felt drawn to her as if to a magnet. Could it be that this exceptionally cultivated young man on his way to a doctorate in political science was not only smitten by the pretty seventeen-year-old typist, but actually pulled into her orbit in the way he had once followed Otto Schneid?

Emily worked at the Central Committee of the KPÖ. She was not only pretty and smart; she seemed to Hugo the very embodiment of the Communist ideal. Her family, as Hugo would soon discover, was poor and working class. When she invited him to stop by the Artbauer apartment, one evening, Hugo was confronted, perhaps for the first time, with true poverty. They lived in one of those apartment buildings, common in the city, which could only be described as gloomy and inadequate in every way.

The first time Hugo entered the building with Emily, he was shocked. There was no electricity, of course, and water only on the landing, where the toilets were located, too. Once inside the apartment, he found himself welcomed by her parents. The father was rather taciturn. He worked at a furniture factory and was a member of the KPÖ. The mother was more lively. She had come, like many of the Viennese working class, from Slovakia, where she had been in domestic service. The father came from Hungary. Both spoke German with exotic accents. Emily's younger sister, Margit, was also home that evening. There was even a lodger living with the Artbauers, who had barely enough room as it was. Such lodgers, only present when night fell and occupying no more space than the bed or couch they slept on, were a normal feature in the living quarters of the poor.

Making his way home that night, Hugo was completely in love with Emily and full of sympathy for her family. He was a boy far from his own family, given to depression and very needy. While his reading, speaking, and writing were those of a sophisticated, worldly adult, his emotional state was a different matter. Here in Vienna, separated from his own home, from his mother, from his beloved woods, he set to work, more or less consciously, building a new identity that would propel him into manhood.

His studies and his relationships with Communist students and with actual revolutionaries like Paul Finder—and now his admiration for young Emily—all contributed to the way he was beginning to position himself in the world. He was now a member of a revolutionary party! Through Helmut Liebknecht he allowed himself to feel connected to the revolutionary history of the Marxist movement. Through Emily, he was learning to value real proletarians. In Paul Finder's reading group, his imagination was turning to the Bolshevik Revolution, to Soviet Russia.

As he headed into the night, having missed the last streetcar, Hugo could hardly have foreseen that his youthful embrace of Communism and his relationship with Emily would result in his expatriation and his lifelong loyalty to the Communist cause. After all, he was barely twenty. He thought of himself as a poet, a writer. He loved music and theater, he was smitten with the glamour of Vienna's *beau monde*, the perfumed, dazzling women in the audiences of the Burgtheater, seen from very high above, where he would stand, enraptured, in the very cheapest standing-room sections. But now, trudging on foot along the city's empty late-night streets, he was heading toward the real world, far removed from the beauty of the operas and symphonies in the brightly lit halls he frequented as a poor relation, so to speak.

He was certainly poor, as were many of his fellow citizens in Vienna that year, and the next one and the one after. In fact, he was beginning to descend into homelessness during the 1921–1922 academic year. At first he had lived with Otto Schneid, in the spacious apartment of Otto's pharmacist uncle. Then he settled for a miserable back room in the two-room apartment of an elderly couple. Eventually he was forced to move to an even worse sublet, sleeping on an old mattress, home to legions of bedbugs. He spent his days at the university, trying to ward off depression. When, at last, Emily found him in his miserable room, she took one look at his surroundings and told him to collect his belongings: he could move in with the Artbauer family.

What kept him from being overwhelmed by self-pity was the weekly telephone conversation with his father, something Papa Huppert had arranged with a family friend in Vienna who had a telephone. And when the summer vacation at last came, Hugo was once again transported, after much chicanery at customs offices, to his beloved Bielitz, where he could recover from the privations of the big city, until, that is, he left again in the fall, returning to Vienna, in spite of the "murderous pain" he experienced upon departure each time. Judging from the many letters from his parents that survive, he kept up a constant epistolary connection with his parents, Mother Anna writing in Polish, Father Huppert in German.

That Hugo was perceived as a difficult person by his parents is clear from some of his father's exasperated letters, including one from May 1922 in which he accused his son of hating his parents, of ignoring his duties to the family, and of showing no gratitude. As Father Huppert saw it, Hugo was a creature of naked egoism. Like so many people with whom Hugo would have dealings in later life, his father noted how quick Hugo was to feel insulted and how easily he reacted with a contemptuous smile. In spite of the obvious pleasures to be found at home in Bielitz, Hugo's visits became rare.

In Vienna, in the course of 1923, hunger and hyper-inflation were making life very difficult. A thick diary reveals what Hugo and Emily experienced that year as they set out for a summer excursion to Salzburg. They were down to their last penny as they witnessed a huge Nazi rally on August 12. Unable to buy even a loaf of bread, they ended up at the back door of a local restaurant, begging for a bowl of soup. They had no way of paying the fare for their return to Vienna. They reached the city of Linz on foot and, once there, they were able to borrow a small sum from local Party members, enough to pay the fare of a Danube passenger ship bound for Vienna.

That year was a particularly difficult one for Emily and Hugo. Emily had lost her job and was trying to find a new one. One of Hugo's Kostufra friends, Stanisław Huberman, who had good contacts at the Soviet Trade Mission, arranged for Emily to be hired there. The result was an immediate improvement in the couple's finances. Emily took shorthand and typed, all the while learning Russian. Her salary went from forty dollars to fifty and eventually to seventy, which in Vienna in 1924 was a fortune. Hugo's dissertation was now in its final stages, ten chapters completed, ready to be moved from his shorthand notes to typewritten pages, thanks to Emily's willingness to do the typing after hours in her office at the Trade Mission (Reisnerstrasse 45).

In 1925 Hugo completed his course work at the university and was looking forward to a year in Paris, where he was to complete his studies with the help of a small stipend, thanks to Professor Kelsen's support. While waiting to leave for Paris, he was supported by Emily. His father was retiring that year and his brother Josef would be studying electrical engineering in Prague. Hugo could no longer count on financial help from home.

His years in Vienna had moved him ever closer to his Communist comrades, especially Helmut, but also Turok (originally Feiner). Paul Finder and the Glaubauf twins were no mere theoretical Communists but militant Party men. Hans Glaubauf would eventually share Finder's fate and die at the hands of the Gestapo. In Vienna, when they were still students, they would meet, some twenty-five or thirty members of Kostufra, in back rooms of various bars and cafes, under the leadership of Stan Huberman, studying and discussing Marxist texts. Huberman, some ten years Hugo's senior, was the younger brother of the world-famous virtuoso violinist, Bronisław Huberman.

Somehow, almost inexorably, the young poet was finding a virtual family among his Communist fellow students. Unlike Finder or Glaubauf, however, Hugo never showed any interest in positions of responsibility or power within the Party. He was a writer and poet above all, and, although he may not have been ready to admit it, his fragile mental health would have stood in the way of an active role in the struggle against fascism. Once he had left his beloved Bielitz behind, separated from his family, his Bielitz girlfriends, and the woods and mountains he loved, he became a nervous wreck, finding equilibrium only in the arms of young women. Writing about a brief encounter with Otto Schneid, in the Vienna of the 1920s, he adopted an elegiac tone, regretting his youth in Bielitz: "How far from us now are those enchanted days."

His dependence on young Emily extended beyond financial support. He thought he could not do without her and he feared her going off to Moscow should the occasion present itself. For that matter, he feared being without her as he prepared for his year at the Sorbonne. When the time came to travel to Paris, alone, he was full of trepidation. Unsure of himself, alone for the first time in his life, worried about being able to live on his meager stipend, he arrived at the Gare de l'Est on December 5, 1925.

The first few days were very difficult. He did not mention this in his published memoirs, but the letters he wrote, addressed to Emily and perhaps actually sent off, in any case preserved in the archives of the Akademie, provide a true picture of this twenty-three-year-old student adrift in Paris. He writes that he had come close to suicide. He tells Emily that he found himself doubting his abilities and even his reason. He suspects that he is of no use to anyone. He begins to doubt whether he really is the writer he claims to be. He acknowledges his hunger for recognition and bemoans the lack of the right connections, his failure to connect with publishers, even his lack of a typewriter. He now finds himself completely alone. He cannot easily communicate with French people. He wishes he could contact the local Communist Party offices, where he would be welcomed, but he lacks the necessary introductions. In sum, he is desperate, lonely, and without prospects. And now, on top of that, he has to deal with Emily's musing about leaving Vienna for Moscow. That is absolute madness, he cries out.

In that wild letter, three things stand out: his dependence on Emily, his reliance on the Communist Party, and his need to be recognized as a writer. The hysterical tone of his letter would be familiar to those who would get to know Hugo in years ahead. In this particular instance, where he gives the impression of being close to a complete breakdown, he may have been portraying his despair in an exaggerated way. In any case, he knew the remedy to his discomfort, the remedy he would turn to throughout his life: find a girl. He tells us about Liline, the young woman he accosted and who was willing to follow him to his hotel room.

He was not really alone and entirely without resources. He had relatives in Paris, including his uncle Emmanuel Huppert, whom he had never met. Uncle Emmanuel, his father's brother, had been living all along with his wife, Paula, in the rue de la Grange Batellière, in a heavily Jewish neighborhood in the Marais. Emmanuel Huppert, who had learned his trade in Germany and found his bride there, was a furrier. The contrast with his brother could not have been starker. Unlike Adolf, the Austrian civil servant, Emmanuel spoke Yiddish and did not cut himself off from his heritage. It was Uncle Emmanuel who provided Hugo with the little he was able to learn about the family his father had seceded from many years ago. Emmanuel and Paula lived very modestly in an apartment which also housed the fur cutting room. Hugo was welcomed there whenever he was hungry, enjoying Paula's home cooking.

And then, of course, there was the Beck family, into which his mother's favorite sister had married many years ago. Hugo's parents had been the guests of their wealthy Parisian relatives, back in 1900, at the time of the great Paris Exposition. Aunt Flora and her husband had raised three children, two of whom, now young men, Sylvain and René, invited Hugo to their impressive apartment in the rue Maubeuge. The occasion was a truly sad one, because the family had been visited by tragedy. Their young daughter, Leontine, had been a victim of the influenza epidemic. Her death devastated the parents, who committed suicide.

There was one more Reich relative in Paris: Margit Reich, the artist. She was the daughter of Uncle Vinzenz Reich, the railway engineer. She lived in Paris, painted, and was welcome in the studios of established painters such as Fernand Léger. She also exhibited in the Salon d'Automne. Hugo had an easy relationship with cousin Margit. In the spring of 1926, he would visit her and her partner in Cagnes-sur-Mer, near Nice, when Emily came over on her vacation and joined Hugo on this excursion to the Mediterranean shore.

It seems clear, then, that Hugo recovered from his original bout of loneliness and self-doubt. He soon improved his French, met other young women, and attended lectures and seminars at the Sorbonne, at least sporadically. He began to frequent the famous cafés of the Left Bank, where he could linger over a cup of coffee while observing the writers and artists who met there. Striking up friendships with women and getting by on very little money allowed Hugo to climb out of his depression, but it was Helmut Liebknecht's arrival in Paris that finally steadied him.

Helmut introduced Hugo to Daniel Renoult, a member of the Central Committee of the French Communist Party who was also an editor of the Party newspaper, *L'Humanité*. This led to offers of employment on a very modest scale, both at the newspaper and at the Secours Rouge, the Communist welfare agency. Hugo found himself welcomed into this closed world. Soon enough he would become a member of the French Communist Party, with the help of Henri Barbusse, the grand old writer who mentored him at the newspaper.

Even though his employment was not quite legal, since, as a foreigner with a student visa, he was not allowed to seek gainful employment, and in spite of the very modest pay, what mattered to Hugo was that he had found a home and a family in the French Communist Party, thanks to Helmut's connections. To speak of a family connection, in this instance, is literally true, since Helmut's grandfather, Wilhelm Liebknecht, had been close to Karl Marx.

Here, in Paris, in 1926, the family connection to the Party's founder was made even more evident when Hugo was introduced to Jean Longuet, the editor of the *Revue Socialiste*. Longuet was Karl Marx's grandson. He had, until recently, been a member of the French parliament. Voluble, amiable, pleased to include his young visitor, Longuet offered to show Hugo around the Palais Bourbon where the parliament was housed. When Hugo showed his pleasure and his appreciation for the old gentleman's offer, Longuet called for the *Revue*'s official vehicle, which turned out to be a splendid 1912 model with leather seats and enormous headlights. They climbed into the famous automobile.

"Cher camarade," said Longuet, "this was the car our comrade Jaurès used almost every day." Jean Jaurès, the Socialist leader who was gunned down on the eve of the war, in 1914, remained a heroic figure for many French citizens. And now, Karl Marx's grandson was taking Hugo along on "the strangest and the most festive ride" of his life. They drove along the Quai des Grands Augustins, the Quai Conti, the Quai Malaquais, the Quai Voltaire, and the Quai d'Orsay, across the river from the Louvre and the Tuileries. Hugo felt completely embraced by the Communist Party.

In the offices of the *Humanité* newspaper and in those of the *Secours Rouge,* administrative changes put into question the meager income assigned to Hugo, but when the money actually ran out, he was saved by a young woman, a Party member, who worked in the *Humanité* offices as a secretary. Her name was Maximilienne, or Maxie for short. Hugo and Maxie formed a strong bond, and the months they spent together were among the happiest Hugo would remember in later years. Maxie had a child, who was living with the grandparents in Brittany. Like Emily before her and a succession of other women in later years, Maxie took care of Hugo, moving into an apartment near the Porte d'Orléans with him. In an unguarded moment, Hugo confessed that he may well prefer Maxie to Emily. After all, Emily was in Vienna and Maxie was right there, offering meals and caresses. Hugo's French was improving by leaps and bounds. He was, for the first time in years, feeling pleased with himself, and he was feeling comfortable in France, more so than in impoverished Vienna. Unfortunately, his residence permit was good for only a year. He had to return to Vienna.

CHAPTER–FIVE

ARRIVING IN VIENNA IN DECEMBER, HUGO WAS MET BY
Emily. She was crying and did not say a word. It seems they agreed to
avoid talking about Hugo's French escapades. They had more important matters to worry about. Hugo needed an income, and he was not
able to find work other than writing for the Communist paper, *Die Rote
Fahne*, which allowed him to hand in an occasional film review and
earn a few pennies. He also worked, again for pennies, for an old friend
of Professor Kelsen's, the economist Walter Federn, who published a
well-regarded weekly, *Der Österreichische Volkswirt*. Federn, who was
Jewish and well informed, advised Hugo to leave the country. There
was no doubt in his mind about what would soon happen: the swastika
crowd was growing by leaps and bounds as unemployment and misery
increased.

The year 1927 would prove to be a time for painful decisions. At the
age of twenty-five, Hugo Huppert was just beginning to be known as a
writer, even if he had not as yet published anything. Witness his invita-
tion to Frau Dr. Schwarzwald's summer artists' colony. He probably
owed this distinction to Professor Kelsen, who participated in one of Dr.
Schwarzwald's many enterprises, the high-level private school for girls.
Genia Schwarzwald knew everyone in Vienna's cultural circles, writers,
artists, composers, philosophers, and opera singers. At her progressive
school for girls, Oskar Kokoschka taught art and Arnold Schönberg
music, among other extraordinary faculty members.

At the Schwarzwald summer colony on the banks of the exquisite Alpine lake, the Grundlsee, famous writers mingled with promising younger aspirants to literary fame. Carl Zuckmayer, Sinclair Lewis, and Rudolf Serkin each stayed there at some point. That summer Egon Friedell, the cultural historian, was among the guests. Hugo had to leave Emily in Vienna and find his way to the celebrated resort for intellectuals. Once there, he lost no time in getting to know major figures such as Friedell. Frau Doktor herself read Hugo's latest poems.

Even as Hugo was beginning his integration into the Viennese literary scene, both he and Emily feared the dark clouds gathering on the horizon. Walter Federn was not alone in expecting dangerous developments, nor was he alone in advising exile. While the labor unions and the Social Democrats were succeeding in their campaign to improve the conditions of the working class, this was also when right-wing reaction, led by Chancellor Ignaz Seipel, was preparing to seize control of the city by force. While Otto Bauer's Social Democrats were winning 63 percent of the vote in Vienna, Seipel was mobilizing troops and seizing weapons stored in the Armory. The fateful confrontation occurred on July 15. The defenseless labor unions faced armed men in uniform. At least 100 were killed, many more wounded.

Hugo managed to miss most of the deadly confrontation, taking refuge in the Soviet embassy and preparing a report on the event for the Russian press. The bloody clash caused him to think ever more seriously about emigration. But the prospect of exile, of being cut off from the German language and from the thriving Viennese literary scene, was too awful to contemplate—especially since he thought that he was beginning to make connections, after all, that summer.

Nevertheless, the events of July 15 pushed him and Emily ever closer to thinking about their safety as well as their living conditions. Hugo was unemployed. For the time being, Emily's wages kept them going. The Soviet Trade Mission had allowed the couple to live in an abandoned mansion on the outskirts of town, but gradually things were becoming ever more difficult. They were eventually forced to retreat to the Artbauer apartment again, and it was becoming clear that the job at the Trade Mission was in jeopardy. By the end of the year the job would vanish. Emily was told that there would be work for her in Moscow, and she could count on a generous severance check and free travel to the Soviet capital.

Could there be work for Hugo in Russia as well? And, to begin with, how could Emily travel, since she had no identity papers at all? While Hugo was an Austrian citizen with a valid passport, neither Emily nor any member of her family had ever possessed proper papers, a not uncommon situation among the poor. Without papers she could not travel to Moscow. What if she married Hugo and if, through marriage, she were to become a citizen? Yes, but without papers, she could not marry.

A friend of Hugo's came up with an unusual solution to the problem: seek the help of Dr. Chajes, the elderly head of Vienna's Jewish community. As it happens, the warm-hearted, cultured old man agreed to welcome Emily into his community, which involved a good many negotiations and a ritual bath, but, finally, on Sunday, January 15, 1928, they were married. Just two weeks earlier, Emily had lost her job at the Soviet Trade Mission. Now, through her marriage to Hugo, she had become an Austrian citizen and would have a passport. With Hugo unemployed and with no means of support, and Emily heading for Moscow where she would try to find work for her new husband, the die was cast. They now had no choice: Moscow was the only possible solution, or so they concluded. Both of them had been depending on the Communist Party ever since they met, when she was seventeen and he was a twenty-year-old student. Now he was twenty-six, she twenty-three.

Emily seems to have taken most everything in stride, but Hugo suffered dramatically from his failures, especially from his failure to find employment after his successful completion of the doctoral program at the university. His return to the wretched poverty of life on the Artbauers' couch, after what had turned out to be a stimulating year in Paris, brought on Hugo's depression once again. Day after day, he awoke from nights in the stifling rooms of the Artbauers' flat with his mind filled with longing for air, for light, and for faraway worlds. On New Year's Eve he collapsed in a drawn-out fit of rage and self-pity. No one wanted his poems. He had nothing and now Emily was prepared to abandon him. He would be alone when she left for Russia. He raged while poor Emily cried, deeply upset by Hugo's behavior.

With the coming of the New Year, Hugo recovered and decided to find new strength in the bosom of his family and to introduce his new wife to his parents, on the eve of her departure for Moscow. He had not been in Bielitz for almost three years and his father had expressed serious doubts about his decision to marry Emily. When the newly-weds arrived in Bielitz, Hugo's depression lifted at last. He was back home and his parents now welcomed Emily, who spent time with her new mother-in-law in the kitchen while Hugo played his piano. He took Emily to his beloved woods, the Zigeunerwald, introducing her to the wintry panorama of his mountain ranges, to the world of his childhood. On Friday evening, Hugo's mother lit the sabbath candles while Emily looked on, full of wonder, and the next day she accompanied the family to the synagogue, where Rabbi Hirschfeld delivered a sermon underlining the Hebrew tradition of openness to all. Later that evening Rabbi Hirschfeld and his wife came to dinner at the Huppert home, together with a local merchant who was the nephew of Rabbi Chajes from Vienna. On Sunday morning Hugo dragged Emily to a surprise visit to his old friend, Erwin Trammer, the musician. Inevitably, the family soon set out to hike in the snow-covered Zigeunerwald, with Emily singing folk songs and Father Huppert delighting in his pretty new daughter-in-law, according to Hugo's recollection. The day culminated in a reunion with several relatives in a hotel restaurant.

On Monday morning the time had come for a tearful departure. They were back in Vienna on Tuesday, and Emily left for Moscow the next day, arriving there on January 27, 1928. Soon she wrote to say that there had in fact been no job waiting for her in Moscow. She was naturally upset and worried. Finding even a couch to sleep on was a challenge and this was a bitter cold winter, in both Vienna and Moscow. Emily, resourceful as usual, soon managed to persuade officials at the Comintern that a German-speaking secretary was just what was needed at their Sixth World Congress. As for Hugo's prospects, here again, Emily showed her resourcefulness: she approached the deputy director of the Marx-Engels Institute, the Hungarian historian Erno Czóbel, speaking in Hungarian and telling him about her husband's qualifications.

Hugo sent his dissertation to Czóbel, who had emigrated from Vienna in 1922. With Emily employed in Moscow and the possibility of employment there for him as well, the familiar pull of Emily's strong personality once again tugged at Hugo, but he admitted to himself that exile was not to be taken lightly. He was obviously worried sick at the thought of leaving the city he was so familiar with, the language that was an essential part of him. Should he, if called, follow his wife into the unknown, the faraway country, with no guarantee of ever seeing his family again? On the other hand, he was desperate to rejoin Emily, while life in Vienna, just then, was becoming unbearable. The best he could do to earn a few *kronen* was to shovel snow for the streetcar company at night and sleep at odd times in the Artbauers' apartment. And that had its own risks and advantages, the chief of those being the presence of Emily's younger sister, Margit.

Hugo could not stand being alone. As he bedded down at night in the small alcove Emily had shared with her younger sister, he was soon attracted to the girl. He noted, in his diary, that he gave her swimming lessons at the public swimming pool and that he was drawn to her as he tried to fall asleep at night across from her. The sight of the girl's bare shoulder and the sound of her soft breathing were enough to precipitate the foreseeable denouement. In his manuscript diary of that year, Hugo noted his growing passion for the girl. He could not resist. The inevitable happened one night, in that stifling, airless alcove.

When a letter from the Marx-Engels Institute's director, David Riazanov, arrived, offering him a conditional appointment, Hugo overcame his fears and hesitations. After all, rejoining Emily and remaining in the Communist world now appeared the only way out, when desperate poverty and the rage of the unemployed made it well-nigh impossible to find a place in the capitalist world which, Hugo believed, was on its last legs. With some help from his parents, he managed to scratch together the fare for the train to Moscow, knowing full well that this was not an ordinary voyage, that it was almost certainly an irreversible move into exile.

His train stopped at the border town of Dieditz, only eleven kilometers from his hometown of Bielitz. He had time to stretch his legs. It was a dark winter night he stepped into. There were no people present, just the scent of earth and snow, and, hidden in the night, the beginning of the highway that led to Bielitz, to his home. Hugo recorded the events of that dark winter night, so close to home, in his diary.

From that fateful moment on he would never be at home; indeed, he would not have a home. His family in Bielitz, with whom, according to his own account, he had had such a blissful reunion in January, would be beyond his reach most of the time and, eventually, would be lost to the Nazi hordes. His room, his piano, his view of the mountains, his wandering in the snow-clad Zigeunerwald, his old school friend Erwin, even the beautiful Lianella Seyfert, to whom he would one day propose marriage—all would recede to accommodate the brutal realities of this deadly century. No wonder that he chose the following motto to describe his life: *Überall nur ein Zugereister* (everywhere only a passerby). On that fateful winter night, when he was so close to home that he could have walked there, he climbed back into his train compartment and continued his journey, past Warsaw and Bialystok, arriving in Moscow in the late afternoon of March 30, 1928.

Emily and Helmut Liebknecht met the train. The spring weather was cold and wet. The streets were dirty and filled with standing water. Hugo's spirits sank. He had imagined his arrival in the Soviet metropolis rather differently. The streetcar turned out to be another foreign experience: nothing like the Paris metro or the Viennese streetcars he was used to. The sheer unyielding mass of people pushing from every direction was not easy to ignore. Emily, noticing Hugo's bafflement, remarked that when the streets were covered in snow it all looked so much better.

The overall surprising impression was that of an impoverished peasant world. The potholed side streets displayed broken down farmsteads, stalls for horses, and other features hard to reconcile with his notion of a world capital. On the main streets, there were houses with windows covered in paper and cardboard. Below them one could see narrow openings leading to cellars and covered with old rags. Here and there, churches in bad repair served the needs of beggars, poor people from the countryside, on their knees before icons and candles. Hugo found it alarming that right in the center of the workers' paradise there were these enclaves of rural, impoverished folk. When he turned to Emily to ask where they would be sleeping that night, her answer was far from reassuring: actually, nowhere. In the two months since her arrival, Emily had not succeeded in finding a place to live. Provisionally, she had arranged to stay with one acquaintance and Hugo with another.

At the institute, Hugo was welcomed by Dr. Czóbel and put to work, in charge of the institute's foreign correspondence. A few days later he was introduced to the "old man" himself, the bearded old revolutionary in charge of the institute, David Riazanov, whose curriculum vitae made Stalin himself look like an amateur. Born in Odessa in 1870, Riazanov, born David Goldendakh, had been a revolutionary since the age of fifteen. He had served several long and hard apprenticeships in Czarist prisons and in exile. Eventually, after another bout of jail time, he settled in London, studying and collecting Marx's and Engels' writings. He worked with Trotsky, publishing in his Viennese paper, *Pravda*. Back in Russia he joined the Bolsheviks but argued for a "democratic communism." He brought his vast collections of Marx and Engels writings to Moscow and founded the Marx-Engels Institute in 1921. Not surprisingly, Hugo, in his memoirs, barely mentions the grand old man who would be arrested as a "Trotskyist" and executed in 1938.

Emily found a sublet, a typical Moscow arrangement. The couple at least had a roof over their heads, even if it was only a tiny space in an apartment shared by three families. The common kitchen, dark and smelly, had no functioning stove or oven. The erstwhile bathroom did not function either; it lacked hot water and the rusty bathtub was used for storage. Later that summer they found better lodgings and, when the World Congress closed its doors, they decided to enjoy a belated honeymoon by traveling to Tashkent, Samarkand, and Bokhara by train. It was during this long excursion, by train, mostly, that their honeymoon turned into tragedy. By the time they reached Baku, on the Caspian Sea, Emily was feverish. In the local hospital she was diagnosed with smallpox. Within days she was dead.

Hugo was inconsolable, completely helpless in the face of this first tragic event of his life. He understood that the dreaded disease, still common in regions such as Uzbekistan and Azerbaijan, infected his young wife because she had never been vaccinated. Father Artbauer would not allow it. At the news of his daughter's death he became so distraught that he talked of hanging himself. Within three years he died, a broken man.

As for Hugo, in the weeks following Emily's sudden death in Baku, his diary entries give the impression that his depression knew no limits. Sitting in a friend's apartment, he castigated himself in a keening rhythm. In the same breath, his diary notations drift in another direction: he wished he could be with his parents. At this point he admitted that he had depended on Emily from the beginning of their relationship. It was Emily who led him into the Communist Party, who gave direction to his incoherent striving. Emily had made him into a healthy person, a comrade, a man.

I would like to linger over these words. This twenty-six-year-old widower, in mourning still for the pretty Viennese girl to whom he owed so much, is of course thinking about himself as he regrets Emily's death. She made him healthy? Yes, to be sure: his depression lifted when he met her. Even though he had been patently unfaithful to her, it was Emily who had made him a man, he wrote in his diary. He was not referring to his sexual coming of age: that had long preceded Emily's arrival on the scene. I think he meant that her influence propelled him into adulthood. Above all, she made him into a comrade. Hugo's entrance into the Communist world certainly owed a great deal to Emily, who had made his departure for Moscow and his entering Riazanov's Institute possible. In Vienna, it was the Soviet Trade Mission that had employed Emily and provided money and lodging for the couple.

There had been other invitations to join Moscow's cause, to be sure. There was Kostufra, the Communist group at the university, with its influential and admired leaders, Helmut Liebknecht above all, but also Vladimir Turok. In Paris, Hugo had been welcomed into the Communist Party in spectacular ways: he owed much to its chief figures in Paris, to whom Helmut had introduced him. He even found himself connecting personally with the Party's past, with Marx's grandson, Jean Longuet, and, through him, with Jean Jaurès, the murdered founder of the French Socialist Party—at least through his surviving automobile.

In those months of 1929 when he was trying to recover from Emily's death, Hugo reached out in different directions. Writing to Maxie in Paris, he declared his undying love to her. He also thought about Emily's young sister, Margit, whom he would have loved to have had by his side at that time. He maintained a steady correspondence back and forth with his father, who was not happy about Hugo's politics and not at all sure that it was a good idea to stay in Moscow. But this was where

Hugo had a salaried position and where he had friends and was able to make new ones.

Among old friends, Helmut Liebknecht, now in Moscow, stood out. Among new friends, the grand prize was the celebrated poet Vladimir Mayakovsky, whom Hugo met shortly before the ill-fated voyage to Samarkand. In Moscow, at this low point in his life, he was consoled by Mayakovsky and found himself welcomed by the poet's lover, Lilya Brik, and her husband, Osip, who was Mayakovsky's publisher. Mayakovsky would soon put an end to his life, but those months when Hugo knew him turned out to be invaluable. He admired the Russian poet's work and tried his hand at rendering it in German adaptation. Eventually, Hugo's German versions of his poems were published and brought him recognition. Through much of his life, Hugo was best known as the preeminent translator of Mayakovsky's work.

As for the Brik household, it proved to be a long-term and invaluable source of support. Lilya Brik, who had grown up, together with her sister Elsa, in a wealthy and cultured Jewish family, was an important figure in Moscow's literary world. Elsa, under the name of Triolet, became a writer in Paris. She would marry the French Communist poet Louis Aragon. In Moscow, Lilya's salon, attended by Mayakovsky's admirers and other influential literary figures, became a welcoming intellectual home for Hugo. More importantly, Lilya herself would remain a comforting friend to Hugo. It was one way in which the young Austrian émigré learned to fit into Moscow society. Already he was beginning to adapt to his new country, improving his Russian, at a time when other Communist intellectuals stranded in this difficult city made little or no progress, speaking mostly to each other. Within a few short years, as Hitler's seizure of power in Germany forced large numbers of writers and artists into exile, Moscow became their temporary home. There they were put to work writing for a number of Comintern publications, including *Internationale Literatur/Deutsche Blätter*, edited by Johannes Becher.

That summer of 1929 was a rare moment of calm before the storms that would soon turn the lives of millions into tragedy. Hitler had not yet come to power and Stalin's dictatorship was still concerned more with building an industrial society than with finding mortal enemies everywhere. Hugo was slowly recovering from the loss of his wife. He had a meaningful and salaried position, friends in Moscow, and the money to travel. Returning to his family for a few weeks was possible. And so he left Moscow to meet with his brother in Vienna before traveling to Bielitz. In Vienna he faced the painful reunion with the Artbauer family, still in mourning for their daughter. Emily's younger sister, Margit, clung to Hugo. He wished he could take her with him, but she did not have the necessary papers.

The Huppert brothers traveled on to Bielitz, where Hugo was able to enjoy simple luxuries absent in Moscow: a hot bath in the morning, eggs for breakfast, clean clothes. The midsummer days were radiant. The family, once again, headed for their beloved Zigeunerwald. Hugo ran into an old flame, the exceptionally beautiful Lianella Seyfert. Would she marry him and join him in Moscow, he asked, between two kisses? This was too difficult a decision for her. Hugo, sitting at his desk half a century later, allowed himself to remark that had she agreed to join him, she would have saved her life. Like almost all the Jewish inhabitants of Bielitz, she would die in Auschwitz.

Hugo's efforts to find a replacement for Emily would soon bear fruit, but his visit home in Bielitz was a time of soul-searching for him. He could hardly have guessed that he would never see his parents again. He was thinking about his place in the world. The decision to leave not only his family but his entire past behind was not yet, in the summer of 1929, necessarily a flight into permanent exile. No one could have foreseen the mass murders set in motion ten years later, although there were already signs of trouble ahead. The political situation in Vienna was not conducive to thoughts of peace. The alliance between the ultra-Catholic chancellor, powerful industrialists, and dangerous armed groups resembling the German Freikorps was paving the way for the elimination of left-wing labor unions. The outline of a fascist state was becoming visible.

Still, having mostly recovered from the privations of the past decade, Vienna was, on the surface, an exciting place. And Bielitz was, as always, truly comfortable, especially when compared to Moscow. Hugo's parents still thought of their son's life in Moscow as a temporary aberration.

They assumed he would return at some point. Hugo, for his part, saw no opportunities in the West, although with Emily no longer at his side, he felt alone and adrift in Moscow when he returned that fall as planned. After all, he had a job there at the Marx-Engels Institute, and a salary.

It would be the spring of 1930 before he found salvation in the person of Vera Smirnova, a young librarian who caught his eye. All at once he threw himself into that feverish state that usually preceded a new sexual conquest. In his diary, at the time, he stopped at nothing in describing his total focus on Vera, the girl he had always wanted, this goddess, his idol. His love for her was limitless! She was twenty-three. Fighting depression, he saw in Vera a powerful tonic, a way of getting back on his feet. Soon there was talk of marriage.

In the course of Hugo's frequent exchange of letters with his father, the discussion now revolved around the decision to marry again. Papa found Hugo's intention to marry a Russian woman disturbing. Clearly, he saw his son moving ever further away from his family and culture. He reminded Hugo of his earlier promise to find a way to be assigned to a post in a European city. He feared that marriage to Vera would widen the abyss already separating father and son. Touched to the quick, Hugo, in his reply, slipped into the feverish language usually confined to his private diary. He explained that he needed Vera, needed her the way one needs air and food. She would make him whole. The marriage went ahead.

Soon after Mayakovsky's suicide, the motives of which Hugo does not allude to in his diary, in the summer of 1930, the newlyweds set out for a honeymoon voyage in the mountainous Caucasus, where Hugo's institute made a summer resort available to scholars and their families in an Alpine setting reminiscent of Switzerland. By train and unreliable bus, they eventually followed the course of the Kuban River, reaching ever higher in sight of the snow-capped mountains. For the first time, Hugo was actually witnessing the terrible disruptions caused by Stalin's collectivization drive: famine and the deportation and execution of very large numbers of farmers. Here, in the land of the Cossacks, resistance to the police and military units charged with the destruction of the kulaks was particularly fierce. Burned-out villages and walls pockmarked with bullet holes could be seen from the bus. Hugo, in his memoirs, would stick firmly to the Party line, denouncing "counterrevolutionary provocations."

Almost automatically, he wrote words of praise for the Five Year Plan, notwithstanding its terrible consequences for the peasantry. Hugo may not have been aware of the mass deportations, the engineered famines, the executions. Perhaps not at the time, but he was writing in the 1970s when Stalin's crimes were no longer state secrets. He glided over the political issues to devote these pages to descriptions of the astonishing landscapes surrounding the Teberda valley, including Europe's highest mountains.

There, the scent of the massive forests induced rapture in the vacationers from Moscow. The sun shone endlessly, and there was tennis and riding as well as conversation with other writers. There was also danger. On the way down to the shores of the Black Sea, the vacationers rode horses, accompanied by armed guards. There was an unmistakable air of fear in the faces of the resort's staff. Hugo wrote of the "serious situation" and of the violent resistance to collectivization in these highlands where every valley squeezed between snowcapped peaks and glaciers was home to ancient ethnic groups, including mountain Jews, fierce, horse-riding people. The horse-mounted academic tourists out of the Teberda resort at last reached the ancient Black Sea harbor city of Sukhumi, with its palm trees and French Riviera climate. Soon they were back in Moscow, returning to their shabby, cramped rooms.

Hugo moved on to study at the Institute of Red Professors, the training ground for Marxist academics. Vera gave birth, in May 1933, to a baby girl they named Annette. While Hugo once again became a graduate student, the international political scene was turned upside down by Hitler's seizure of power in Berlin that January. Within the Soviet Union, 1933 was the year of the completion of the first Five Year Plan and the death, by starvation or firing squad, of entire populations, in the Ukraine especially, and in Kazakhstan. Stalin's wife, Nadhezda, with whom Hugo claims to have spent time in a library at the Marx-Engels Institute, died of a gunshot wound to her heart on November 7, 1932, the anniversary of the October Revolution. The official cause of her death was said to be appendicitis, even though a gun was found next to the body. Suicide? Murder? Two doctors who refused to sign the death certificate—presumably unconvinced by the official explanation—were eventually arrested and shot.

None of these developments were able to shake Hugo's firm conviction that the Party could do no wrong. He was hardly alone in sticking to the Party line, no matter how absurd it might have been. The Ukrainian genocide was kept secret, even as multitudes—men, women, and children—were shipped to concentration camps in Siberia and other distant, hidden locations. At the same time, the Nazi threat was making it ever more difficult to adopt a critical attitude toward the Soviet state. This was true both of Soviet citizens and of outsiders. Few had the inside knowledge and the courage of Franz Borkenau, whom Hugo knew briefly in Vienna. Borkenau, who was an official of the Comintern, resigned his post in 1929. He was one of the earliest defectors who understood the police state Stalin was creating. Other observers, including Arthur Koestler, did not discover the dark side of the Soviet state for several more years.

With all this in mind, Hugo's blind attachment to the Soviet Union is understandable, especially in the harrowing years leading up to the war. As he explains in his memoirs, he was intent on fitting in successfully in his Russian milieu, but he never thought of his future as anything but temporary exile. His ultimate goal was to return to Vienna once the fascists were defeated—not a very likely prospect in the 1930s. Although reports from the Spanish Civil War by observers such as George Orwell and Borkenau were opening the eyes of some thinking people to the vicious effects of Stalin's policies, within the Communist sphere no doubts were permitted: the truth was whatever the Party said it was, at any given moment.

In Moscow, the crowd of refugee intellectuals kept growing. Many were well-known figures, writers with international reputations, whose books were soon to be consigned to the flames in Nazi Germany. As Hugo was quick to point out, his own position among the well-known exiles who were greeted on arrival with flowers and marching bands was that of a nobody. He had no books, no prizes, no reputation. He had reached Moscow thanks to his enterprising young wife. He was there to escape the misery of Vienna in the 1920s.

What he had going for him was his friendship with Helmut Lieb-knecht, who entered the Kremlin fortress, Stalin's Forbidden City, at will. Through Helmut he was known to Sonia Liebknecht and to other luminaries among the exiles, such as Clara Zetkin, who had represented the German Communist Party in the Reichstag. Hugo's marriage to a Russian woman, his increasing fluency in the Russian language—rare among the better-known refugees housed in the Hotel Lux—and, now, his three-year commitment to the Institute of Red Professors all brought him much closer to successful assimilation than was the case with the A-list exiles.

His trump card, his cherished ace, was his Party membership card: number 1792910, handed to him on November 30, 1930, once he had completed the necessary paperwork to transfer his membership from the Austrian and French parties to the Soviet one. His diary entries from the winter of 1930 are filled with jubilation. He was now a member of the Russian Communist Party. There were also practical advantages: he had become eligible, for instance, to apply for a stipend from the Institute of Red Professors.

Enrolled now as a "political culture worker," he was sent on a six-week mission to coal mines worked by German-speaking miners. He recorded his impressions in his diary. Those diaries were meant as the raw material of future novels. He did, in fact, plan to write a novel set in the violent aftermath of the last war, in 1918 and 1919, in Bielitz and Teschen, but his plan fell through, in part because his Party obligations kept him busy.

That mission in the coal mining district, many hours away, in slow-moving and overcrowded trains, led to new experiences for Hugo, including sleigh rides in bitter cold weather, the only available transportation in the snow-covered fields leading to the mines. Once there, he was settled in one of the seventy-five barracks and introduced to the miners he was sent to enlighten. They were Germans, from the Ruhr, and not especially primed for cultural propaganda. Hugo's efforts may not have helped to sway the rowdy, beer-drinking miners, but his meticulous notes led to the publication, in Russian translation, of one of his earliest reportages.

The next step in his literary career was initiated by the editor of the Party's newspaper, *Izvestia*. Ivan Gromov, who had succeeded Bukharin in the post, wanted to send a team of professional writers to the Siberian coal mines of the Kuznetz basin where they would be embedded with the miners long enough to guarantee authenticity in their reports. Hugo joined several colleagues chosen for this expedition in the summer of 1933. They traveled under awful conditions on the Trans-Siberian Express to the Tomsk station where they switched to a local train heading for the mines. Along the way, they sent dispatches to their editors. They must have passed freight trains filled with Ukrainian peasants, starving victims of the Five Year Plan deported to Siberian labor camps.

That summer's dispatches to *Izviestia* led to the publication of Hugo's first book, a German-language reportage about the Siberian mines, under the title of *Sibirische Mannschaft*. It was Erich Wendt, then deputy director of Vegaar, the publishing arm of the Comintern's foreign language propaganda efforts, who counseled Hugo and published the book. Wendt probably knew Hugo in Vienna, where he had been in charge of another Party publishing enterprise. He reached Moscow in 1931, together with his wife, Charlotte, and joined the elite of refugee Party stalwarts.

Hugo's book was simultaneously published in Moscow and Zürich, as well as in New York, in English translation, in 1934, under the title *Men of Siberia*. This book, which is now on my desk, is a colorful snapshot of what the man was thinking, of what he was hiding, of what he felt he had to write, since this was clearly a blunt piece of Comintern propaganda meant for the outside world.

The book reached publication at a particularly tense moment in the political life of the Soviet Union. Hitler had just come to power in Germany. The Great Depression hung over the Western countries like a dark cloud. Unemployed workers from Germany and other hard-hit regions did find work in the Soviet Union, which was building the infrastructure for an industrial economy at breakneck speed while expropriating peasants by the hundreds of thousands and herding them into collective farms under threat of deportation and arrest. The first Five Year Plan had just been completed. Its victims were facing starvation, deportation, slave labor camps, and executions.

It is against this backdrop that the enormous propaganda machine of the Communist Party sent writers to places like the Kuznetz basin in Siberia, to document and extoll the achievements of the Soviet Union and to contrast these with the failures of the capitalist economies. Hugo's book is propaganda, but also first-rate reportage. It introduces the colorful, personal, dramatic story-telling technique of the Viennese newspapers into what would otherwise be mere factual reporting—so many tons of steel, such exceptional results. The most famous practitioner of this kind of reporting was probably Egon Erwin Kisch, whom Hugo admired and with whom he conferred when he was in Berlin. Hugo's own "poetic reportage" first reached a large audience in this first book, *Men of Siberia*.

The book begins with a snapshot of the commotion at the Moscow railroad station as trains prepare to leave for Siberia: soldiers are heard swearing, women are crying, one hears iron chains clattering. All this exceptional noise spills over into the carriages filled with prisoners. As the train starts moving, one could hear the cries of the women, the mothers and sisters. They were sure that their menfolk would never return from faraway, unimaginable Siberia.

Here Hugo is actually citing an account written by A. Shapalov, around 1898, which I am paraphrasing. It never seems to occur to Hugo or to his editor that this description of Siberian deportations in Czarist Russia, written some thirty-five years earlier, is hardly different from daily experiences in 1933, except that the prisoners now are poor peasants, not revolutionaries and intellectuals, such as Fyodor Dostoyevsky, and that the awful experience takes place on a much larger scale.

When Hugo's train lumbers out of the station and picks up speed, he looks out of the compartment's windows and sees innumerable watchtowers manned by Red Army soldiers holding guns—and masses of laborers below, digging under guard. Passengers explain who the unfortunate laborers are: they are said to be kulaks, "men who had been exploiters, enemies of the Soviet State, arsonists and bandits." Lest his readers show signs of feeling sorry for them, we are told, perhaps not very convincingly, that the men could be seen smoking, laughing, and carrying on conversations.

To point out that, compared to workers in America, those peasants were much better off, Hugo has an American engineer traveling in the same compartment assure his listeners that if those prisoners digging ditches along the path of their train were in America, "along the Hudson and the islands," they would not be laughing. Why bring in the kulaks at all? Could it be that our "poetic reporter" is quietly subverting his report? There is absolutely no reason to question his motives, to wonder whether he sees the pain, the injustice, the horror of Stalin's policies, which resulted in the willful destruction of so many lives in the years of the first Five Year Plan. Nevertheless, we ought to be on the lookout for hesitations in the work of this complicated man.

Arriving in Siberia, in the mining town renamed Stalinsk, he describes an "ochre-colored mass of dust that stood out against the afternoon sky, as big as a mountain. It was composed of a thousand smaller columns leaning in the wind, like a forest of transparent trees. At the foot of this mountain of dust, one could see an entire town. A most unusual town." Hugo reports on the gigantic industrial process, but he makes it all very personal, engaging in conversations with all kinds of people. Here, for instance, is his political caricature of a man suspected of harboring unworthy thoughts, a man named Shtuprin, dog trainer by profession. Shtuprin comes to life on a page illustrated with a line drawing of a short, fat, cigar-smoking man, a caricature of an enemy of the people that could have come straight from the pages of the vile Nazi publication *Der Stürmer.*

Our reporter is having a chat with a worker and his family when "a short, fat man enters the room without knocking." He is introduced as "Mr. Shtuprin, our dog trainer." The newcomer corrects the introduction: "Excuse me, excuse me: Comrade Shtuprin, chairman of the dog training center in Novosibirsk." We then discover that Comrade Shtuprin had been a POW during the last war in Germany, where he learned his dog-training skills. At that point, Shtuprin goes on to say: "What an idiot I was! I should have stayed there. Nothing happens here. In winter, wolves dance around the town. You tell me there are eight million unemployed workers in Germany? And we here have no unemployment? Come on, in Germany every beggar is like a Count, compared to our people here. The last time I was in Moscow on business I kept throwing coins into the hats of hungry, begging men." At this point Shtuprin gets carried away with his denunciations of Soviet life: "And what about the 100,000 peasants torn away from their homes, is that a joke perhaps?" The fat, cigar-chomping Shtuprin is an obvious villain. He is contrasted with pretty young Nadhezda, who happened to be in the room when Shtuprin uttered his comments. She was furious and quietly mentioned that she heard that new efforts were being made to uncover counter-revolutionary talk. Hugo moves on.

In August, he traveled with a colleague to Old Kuznetz. The dilapidated bus crawled through the hot, silent steppe until it reached the banks of a great river that promised relief from the heat. The tourists from Stalinsk then swim in the river, between masses of tree trunks moving with the current. Crossing the river, the travelers reached the old town, swathed in the shade of many trees. The town was an anachronism for those used to the hustle and noise of Stalinsk. Here quiet reigns; there are no straight lines, just a hillside covered with gardens and houses hidden under the shade of oaks. From the meandering streets one could see silent people sitting on porches around their samovars. Laundry is drying on clotheslines between the houses. Church bells can be heard ringing, and high above the town one can see the ruins of the ancient citadel.

Into this quiet summer scene, Hugo suddenly introduces a memory of winter. On a winter evening of the year 1857, a passenger alights from the postal sleigh, wrapped in furs. He is Fyodor Dostoyevsky. Condemned to death, pardoned, banished to Siberian exile, he is now, after nine years of suffering as a prisoner, allowed to travel to marry the woman he loves. The couple lived in Old Kuznetz for a year before getting permission to return to Moscow. The simple house where they lived is now preserved and the street named Dostoyevsky Street. This is where Dostoyevsky wrote *The House of the Dead*.

Hugo owed the publication of his Siberian book to Erich Wendt. In Wendt, Hugo found an effective patron. In the postwar years, Wendt would move back to Berlin, together with the entire cadre of exiles who had spent the war in the Soviet Union. This close-knit group of Party executives was sent to run the Soviet-occupied part of Germany. Wendt's wife went on to marry Walter Ulbricht, the East German head of state, and Wendt himself presided over the Aufbau Verlag, the chief publishing house of the East German Communist State (Deutsche Demokratische Republik [DDR]). What Hugo never mentions is that Wendt also traveled to Siberia in 1937 as Stalin's purges were reaching their climax. Wendt was deported to the Gulag and not freed until the outbreak of the Great Patriotic War.

Such omissions, paired with wildly inflated words of praise for his sponsors, are found throughout our author's oeuvre. It serves as a caution for biographers, although one needs to acknowledge that Hugo's selective discretion, with an eye on the censors and the Soviet security apparatus (Narodnyy Komissariat Vnutrennikh Del [NKVD]), was the norm in the Communist world. The German-language publications out of Moscow, including *Das Wort*, edited by Willi Bredel, could count on editorial boards that included well-known writers such as Bertolt Brecht and Lion Feuchtwanger. Bredel was another member of the Hotel Lux elite and one more of Hugo's patrons who would eventually appear on an East German postage stamp. Hugo's editor-in-chief at the monthly *Internationale Literatur / Deutsche Blätter*, Johannes R. Becher (Comrade Hans), an older, well-known poet and novelist, came under suspicion, but he would eventually rise to great heights. In postwar Berlin, Becher succeeded Arnold Zweig as head of the Akademie der Künste and served as minister of culture of the DDR. Hugo was Becher's deputy in Moscow, and he paints a somewhat mixed picture of his boss, who clearly did not think much of him. Needless to say, there is no mention, in Hugo's memoirs, of Becher's fall from grace and of his later rehabilitation.

One could almost explain those silences by the routine nature of the ups and downs of life under Stalin's dictatorship. Wendt and Becher were indeed rehabilitated, but most outcomes were bloodier. The famous old Bolsheviks who were tortured and killed included Riazanov, Hugo's superior at the Marx-Engels Institute, and Bukharin, the editor of *Izvestia*. These were dangerous times, culminating in the show trials of 1938.

Hugo's discretion, when writing about the fates of Stalin's victims, contrasts sharply with his openness about his innumerable seductions. Whether he was married to Emily or to Vera, he goes on record with pleasurable recollections of the young women he steers into his bed, including one-night stands in the countryside. In his view, marital fidelity is a bourgeois notion that cannot be binding on a genuine Communist. Don Giovanni was born too soon.

The profiles and sketches devoted to the writers Hugo met in Moscow included not only exiles such as Willi Bredel, but Russian writers of the 1930s who were on the way to becoming an endangered species. There was Mayakovsky, of course, whom Hugo admired immensely. There was also Isaak Babel. Babel was arrested and tortured in 1939 and executed shortly afterward. Hugo's sketch of Babel at a cocktail party rings true. Babel sat in a corner, Hugo remembers, got up to check out his host's library shelves, picked out a volume, and started reading. Avoiding most of the conversations, he poured cognac in his tea, ate some cold herring salad, drank a glass of seltzer, and left. His hosts knew perfectly well that all the posturing—the clichés, the perfumed cigarettes, the trimmed beards, not to mention the presence of young ballerinas—meant nothing to Babel, who headed home to his wife along the snow-covered streets. It is in connection to Babel that Hugo allows himself an uncharacteristic remark about the "gruesome, undeserved" fate Babel suffered.

Hugo himself did not escape arrest at the height of Stalin's purges. They came for him on the very day of Hitler's takeover of Austria, March 12, 1938. He does not say much about the time he spent in prison, more than a year. He must have been denounced and, in the course of the brutal interrogations he experienced, it would not surprise me if he, in turn, denounced others. It was only his return from prison that he wrote about. It was at night, the night of April 28–29, 1939, that he emerged from the prison's gates, thin and unshaven, waiting for a streetcar, which arrived at last, almost empty. The conductor noticed Hugo's threadbare clothes and the bag out of which his wooden spoon stuck out. It was clear to him what kind of passenger this was. The conductor smiled good-naturedly and refused payment.

Instead of feeling joy and anticipation, Hugo felt only estranged, deeply estranged. He felt he no longer belonged and he wanted to shriek into the night. When he reached his house and knocked on the gate, there was Vera's mother, making the sign of the cross. Reintegration was difficult. Vera had changed, and not for the better, according to Hugo. His old job as Becher's deputy was no longer available. Fortunately, he was welcomed and helped by Lilya Brik. And then his institute sent him, together with wife and child, to a summer-long vacation in Yalta.

In late August, returning from his vacation, he was greeted with one of the most shocking political developments of his life. Hitler's emissary, Ribbentrop, had just landed in Moscow. This was the latest and most surprising twist in Stalin's foreign policy. It resulted in the non-aggression pact with Hitler and the secret agreement to partition Poland. Moscow's airport was decorated with swastikas!

That particular pirouette in the Party's ever-changing stance would have been very hard to swallow. In the course of the brief interlude of the Popular Front, the Social Democratic parties of western Europe, including the French Socialist Party, had gone from being labeled "Social Fascists" to being embraced as comrades in an "anti-fascist" coalition against Hitler's Germany. Now, suddenly, on August 23, 1939, Stalin was prepared to join Hitler in his campaign against Poland. It was Stalin's close confidant, Molotov, who negotiated the public and the secret agreements, after Stalin, to please Hitler, had removed Litvinov, who was Jewish, from his post as foreign minister. I can imagine what Hugo was thinking and what he could not openly say, even if he did not know about the secret codicil to the pact between the two dictators: Stalin had just signed the death decree of Poland's Jewish population. Within a week, on September 1, 1939, German motorized units drove into Bielitz and Teschen, murdering along the way, while local ethnic Germans celebrated their arrival. All of Hugo's—and my own—relatives were doomed.

At this point, having heard from his brother, Hugo starts thinking about visiting him in Lemberg (Lwów), where Josef and his young wife, Lilian, had taken refuge after fleeing the German advance. Lwów and the western Ukraine were "liberated," as Hugo puts it, when the Red

Army moved into previously Polish territory on September 17, in accordance with the secret protocols of the Molotov-Ribbentrop Pact. It now became possible for a Soviet citizen to travel to Lwów without crossing borders. Hugo does not dwell on what happened on September 1, when German troops seized his hometown. The Jewish population of Bielitz and of its neighbor, Teschen, was "liquidated," as the Nazis liked to say. Hugo's mother was no longer among the living, but everyone he had known almost since birth was gone all at once.

By the time Hugo could free himself to travel to Lwów, it was June 1941. The city was now part of the Soviet Union, so travelers could easily get there by train. He arrived on June 18 and spent six days in the city. He wrote down his experiences later that year and presented the result, almost unedited, in a long and remarkable section of his memoirs. He began by describing the train's slow approach to Lwów and noted his Russian fellow passengers' curiosity, as they saw a European city for the first time. Instead of the familiar wooden houses, they saw solid buildings built of stone, a cityscape familiar to anyone from Vienna, Berlin, or Budapest but entirely new to the eyes of travelers from the East.

Hugo was anxious. He had not seen his brother in twelve years. Would he be meeting the train? Would he even recognize his brother? In the streetcar taking him to his brother's address, he watched the half-ruined façades of houses and churches that had come under artillery fire when the Germans shot up the city or when the Soviets did, at some point. Hugo had not been in Lwów in twenty years. His last visit was with his uncle, Vinzenz Reich. Now he could enjoy the familiar sights of a European city: front yards behind ironwork fences, clean and well-maintained sidewalks, the festive old Austrian post office. He was pleasantly surprised by all these signs of European normalcy. When he reached his destination, at number 47 Lyczakowska Street, the neighborhood reminded him of Vienna; everything seemed familiar. He knocked on the door and was welcomed by a woman who led him to a table where his breakfast awaited him. Somehow his brother had missed him at the train station.

Hugo spoke with an elderly barber who knew German about what happened in 1939, when the German military surrounded the city and then, at the last moment, retreated as the Red Army approached. There was jubilation in the streets, but later. . . . What then, Hugo asked? The barber suddenly became unfriendly and would say no more.

Hugo enjoyed a bath in the attractive modern bathroom and, after breakfast, he continued to marvel at everything in sight: the comfortable European apartment houses across the street, with maids airing out blankets and pillows and making beds, sweeping and putting everything in order. A forgotten world, Hugo exclaimed, clearly feeling the strong pull of his homeland. Even the sidewalks, warmed by the morning sun, seemed to give out an "un-Russian" aroma. The chestnut trees, even the dust, carried familiar scents. When he picked up the telephone at the nearby post office and put a call through to Josef's factory, he heard his brother's voice and the familiar Bielitz accent. This was music to his ears.

He was now in the grip of nostalgia. A life broken in half is unbearable, he thought, taking himself back to the year 1928, when he had left for Moscow and when Emily died. He thought about the death of his parents, whom he last saw in the summer of 1929, and he thought about his brother's flight and his own hellish life in prison: and now he was about to reconnect with his brother and with his own past. After all those years away from home, from the familiar scenes of his childhood, he now hungered for the West and the "damned old Austria" of the past.

This was June 18: the weather was splendid and the people in the streets seemed happy. Radio broadcasts out of London were warning of German troop movements and an imminent attack, but who would take this seriously? After all, the German-Russian non-aggression pact of 1939 was still intact, even while Hitler's armies were busy in the west and England remained alone. *Pravda* and Moscow Radio had just explained that the German troop movements were harmless maneuvers. War seemed far away, and the sun was shining.

Hugo reached the weekly market in front of the courthouse. Among the shoppers, he could see well-dressed, urbane Polish ladies, next to Ukrainian peasants in traditional dress and silent Jews in black caftans. A little to the side he observed mountain folk sitting on potato sacks, and, everywhere, pretty village girls. It all evoked feelings of home for Hugo. Joining the crowd of shoppers, he bought a bundle of radishes and entered a pastry shop of the kind he used to patronize at home. Several Red Army soldiers were inside the shop, asking for sandwiches and beer. The Jewish shopkeeper treated the Soviet soldiers contemptuously, pretending not to understand Russian and joking in Yiddish with his assistant at the expense of the Russians. Hugo was outraged and yelled at the man in German. Poor idiots, he thought to himself, shady merchants disappointed by the Soviet presence.

He continued his nostalgia tour: how close to home he was, even if it was out of reach. How un-Russian everything was here. Later in the day, he visited with a Polish writer, Stanislaw Lec, in the local writers' club, establishing connections with the intention of spending a month in town. Shortly before five in the afternoon he arrived at the gates of the factory where his brother worked. They met at last and tried to catch up. Josef explained how he and Lilian fled Bielitz, a step ahead of the Nazi troops. They left seventy-five-year-old Adolf Huppert, who was in poor health, in the care of Lilian's mother. Anna Huppert died in 1936. When they finally managed to reach Lwów, under Russian occupation ("liberation," in Hugo's vocabulary), they had to find a way of making a living in the overcrowded city, filled with refugees and Soviet troops.

Hugo was aware that they lived in poverty, even though they were both employed. Lilian worked as a kindergarten teacher. Hugo was thinking of ways of bringing his brother and sister-in-law to Moscow. He continued to suffer from homesickness, amplified by his surroundings and his reunion with his brother. Hearing that Olga Langer, Otto Schneid's erstwhile girlfriend, was in town brought back memories of his Bielitz youth. The brothers talked about their childhood, their home, their parents, fully aware that all this was lost for good. Silently, they evoked the lost house on the Tuchmachergasse, the shade of the Zigeunerwald. They switched to a discussion of travel plans as they ate their supper. Columns of armored vehicles thundered past. There were rumors in the city about an imminent German attack. A number of Jewish families had already left, heading east.

On that weekend in Lwów, Hugo's attempts to reconnect with his past fell short. He tried to find Bella, the girl he was kissing when she was seventeen. Married, she now was living in Lwów, but he could not locate her that day. As for Uncle Vinzenz, his mother's favorite brother, the railway engineer, he actually saw him that Saturday. Uncle Vinzenz was not very forthcoming. He resented the Soviet authorities who had removed him from his post. He was obviously not in sympathy with the new order. His daughter, Margit, the painter, whom Hugo had known in Paris, was in town, too. Hugo planned to visit with her the next day. He reached Olga Langer by telephone, but he did not feel particularly welcome there, either.

That evening he was scheduled to speak at a memorial event for Clara Zetkin, which he did, speaking in German to an audience of local writers who for the most part understood him. "I said what needed to be said and stayed away from all the forbidden words and names." This candid reference to Party censorship is a rare admission. The "forbidden names" included, of course, a legion of revered revolutionaries, Bukharin, Babel, Riazanov, and so many others who had been executed on Stalin's orders. Hugo allowed himself to think more freely than he would in Moscow, in the shadow of Stalin's prisons. In June 1941, in Lwów, in his brother's company, his whole being was suffused with thoughts of home, of family, of Europe. More than ever he was feeling exiled in the Soviet universe. He went to bed muttering half-forgotten Polish words from his childhood.

Sunday morning he awoke early. His brother was standing at the open window in his pajamas. Lilian was sitting up in bed. They were both listening intently to new sounds in the distance. Guns, still far away, were getting louder. Anti-aircraft fire. Surely only practice shooting, said Hugo. Lilian joined the two men at the window. "There is a line of women in front of the bakery, before seven in the morning. Now I know. It is war," said Lilian.

A knock on the door. The Polish landlady entered. "The war has started," she said, quietly adding: "Jesus Maria." From the street they could hear someone saying, loudly, in Yiddish: "In Shitomir they already are." In the blue summer sky, puffs of smoke appeared. Down below, in the street, people were running past. On the balconies, half-dressed men and women stared at the goings on in the sky. Lilian ran downstairs to stand in line for bread. Women were crying. One neighbor looked at Hugo and yelled at him: "You are still here? Don't you know what is happening? Run, right now, run to the train station, there may still be trains leaving town, at any moment it may be too late!"

Josef now joined in. "We have to change our plans, Hugo. You need to go back to Moscow, quickly. I need to stay with the factory." Hugo picked up his papers, money, and a slice of bread and dropped it all in his briefcase. In the street, he could see abandoned streetcars. He then tried to reach Party headquarters. The Party was his protector. He phoned the Party office: no one answered. It was Sunday, after all. He started to walk toward the train station, thirsty, exhausted. He convinced himself that he was not abandoning his brother, whose calm advice seemed right to him: everyone in his own place. Josef's place was at work, Hugo's in Moscow.

Making his way along the main boulevard to the train station, he ran into a Jewish writer whom he had met at the Zetkin memorial. The man smiled, extending his hand. Where was he going? To Sambor, where his wife and children were waiting for him. Did he not realize that the German advance must have reached the town? And that his wife and child were probably dead by now? Having sent off a telegram to his own wife in Moscow, he touched the greeting card signed by his daughter which he carried in his breast pocket and looked up to see a squadron of Russian fighter planes in the sky. All at once he felt secure. He stepped into the barbershop in the train station and asked to be shaved. There was a line in front of the window where tickets were sold. The window was closed, however. Were there seats for the train to Moscow, and would there be a train today? No one knew. Rumors abounded. Now a formation of black German attack planes could be seen over the rooftops. Machine guns fired at them. The waiting crowds dispersed in an instant. In the distance, black smoke rose where German bombs had landed.

On the street, wounded men and women, covered in blood and the white chalk dust created by the collapse of walls, were running away from the bombs' impact. Broken glass was underfoot everywhere, and broken bodies lay on the ground. The street smelled of blood and smoke. A house was on fire nearby. Hugo returned to his brother's apartment. They argued, once again, about staying or leaving. Hugo must go, Josef must stay.

As they talked, they saw trucks down below, loaded with fleeing Russians headed east, afraid of the Ukrainian population even more than of the Germans. In the sky, heading in a northwesterly direction, another German bomber squadron could be seen. On the landing, an elderly Jew was praying. He turned to Hugo and said, in Yiddish: "The Germans, when they come, they will kill us." On the street, horse-mounted militia men galloped by. The stores were all closed down.

Monday morning, the bombing continued. After trying everything else, Hugo decided to walk as far as the suburban station where trains leave for Russia, under normal conditions. It was a very long walk in the summer heat. When he reached the station, he found that it had been bombed. It was now surrounded by craters. Ticket office? Forget it, said the man next to him. No more tickets. Two passenger trains, not moving as yet, had become the crowd's target. People threw away their suitcases. The train's compartments were full. Hugo pushed his way into the nearest one. His luck held out: a Ukrainian mother made room for him. At last the train started to move.

Those nerve-racking six days in June tore away at Hugo's convictions. At first, under the spell of a city filled with familiar sights, a city that had been part of the prewar Austrian world that spelled home for Hugo, he could not help comparing his surroundings to his life in Moscow. The reunion with his brother strengthened his feeling of being back in Europe—back home, in a way. And then, as the bombs started falling, as war began, he suddenly retreated to the only safety he knew now that the Germans, who had already destroyed the world he knew, from Bielitz to Vienna and Paris, were about to enter Lwów. Nothing was left now, no home in the West, no solace offered by family: only Moscow, only the Party, and his Russian wife and child.

CHAPTER—SIX

ON JUNE 22, 1941, HITLER'S ARMIES, SOME THREE MILLION strong, invaded the Soviet Union. Millions of men, women, and children were about to die, as soldiers, prisoners, and victims of bombardments and murderous assaults by Nazi death squads and Ukrainian armed gangs. Hugo witnessed the unfolding of this vast tragedy in Lwów that same day. Abandoning Josef and Lilian to their fate, he managed to save himself, just barely, and return to his family in Moscow after a grueling train ride lasting several days, in constant danger from aerial bombardments.

Back in Moscow, he was assigned to a propaganda unit producing leaflets and broadcasts aimed at German troops. Whatever hesitations he may have had since his prison time about staying in Russia, now that war had started he was inevitably throwing in his lot with the Soviet Union. He may have been feeling exiled in this vast land, so fundamentally different from the Europe he remembered. He clearly felt the difference in Lwów on those spectacular summer days in June, but the attraction of the familiar could not compete with the sudden, fundamental need for security. Europe was in the hands of murderers. Only the Red Army offered resistance.

While Hugo stayed in Moscow for the time being, Vera and Annette were evacuated to Chistopol, on the Kama River, in the Soviet Far East. Unsurprisingly, Hugo took advantage of the situation, getting together with an attractive young woman who moved in with him for a while. Another young woman soon followed, a student whom he called Lara. In her single room, on the fifth floor, while they were talking and drinking, sirens shrilled and bombs started falling. Instead of descending into the cellar, Lara pulled the curtains shut and started taking her clothes off.

This little interlude, with Hugo wifeless in Moscow under bombardment, ended when the last Comintern propagandists were evacuated to the Tatar republic, in Chistopol, where Vera and Annette were already established. The small town on the Kama River was to become home to dozens of writers and their families. Mayakovsky's mother and sisters were among the Hupperts' neighbors. Arriving in the late fall of 1941, with snow already on the way, the evacuated writers found themselves in a remote place, with wooden planks running along the one shopping street. The ambiance resembled scenes from a Wild West film, except that the streets were named after Liebknecht, Rosa Luxemburg, and Engels. Electricity was scarce. Conversations among the well-known writers, Russian and foreign, including Boris Pasternak, continued into the night, in poorly illuminated rooms and around steaming samovars. Behind windows covered in ice, the houses smelled of pine wood, bread dough, and smoke coming from stoves and ovens.

With the coming of spring, the paths became thick with mud. Lilac bushes blossomed, and so did the cherry trees, when, at last, orders came from Moscow: the time had come to return to the capital, as German forces were in retreat. Hugo celebrated his fortieth birthday in Chistopol before his departure for Moscow. Wife and child were still expected to stay away. When they at last returned to Moscow, Hugo was drafted for propaganda work with German prisoners in a camp some 300 kilometers to the north. He was part of a team that included Leo Stern, who had been a student of Kelsen's and Grünberg's in Vienna. Stern had fought in the Spanish Civil War and would become, after the war, rector of the Martin Luther University in Wittenberg and vice president of the Academy of Sciences in East Germany. Vasile Spiru, whom Hugo had known as a fellow member of Kostufra in his student days in Vienna, also joined the team. He would eventually become a professor of history at the Karl-Marx University in Leipzig. Otto Braun, who had fought in China and who would, after the war, become First Secretary of the Writers' Union in the DDR, served with Hugo, teaching the German contingent, while

Leo Stern took care of the Austrian prisoners. Spiru worked with the Rumanians and "Comrade Luigi," a relative of the Italian Communist leader, Togliatti, took responsibility for the Italian prisoners.

The foresight of the Soviet authorities, focusing on the future and the reeducation of enemy soldiers in the midst of bloody battles, was in stark contrast to the German approach which, simply put, organized the death by starvation of millions of Russian prisoners. The Red Army's experience with the political indoctrination of its own troops provided a solid background for the indoctrination of enemy prisoners.

Hugo did not do so well in his first assignment. The camp was surrounded by woods. There was no escape from living day after day among thousands of prisoners, all men. Depression threatened, encouraged by the absence of female company. Hugo asked to be sent to the front. Instead, his superiors transferred him to another prisoner camp, the Antifascist Central School in Krasnogorsk, within easy reach of Moscow. Here the instructors could commute on weekdays and spend their weekends in Moscow. The vans taking instructors to the school occasionally carried Comintern eminences, men like Walter Ulbricht, Maurice Thorez, and Palmiro Togliatti.

Hugo's depression, which had become especially acute after he completed his assignment in the prisoner camps, led him to seek psychiatric help. He wrote very little about this experience. He accepted a new assignment in the summer of 1944 as private secretary to Ilya Ehrenburg, who was, in many ways, the man Hugo would have wanted to be. A poet, novelist, war correspondent, and friend of major artists in prewar Paris, he was a powerful figure, always on the move, heading for the front. He reported from the front lines of the Spanish Civil War in the late 1930s and now from the war against Hitler.

He was Jewish and had been imprisoned and exiled by the Czarist police and also the Soviet secret police. He was a childhood friend of Bukharin, but he was also close to the artists and poets of the 1920s: Picasso, Modigliani, and others who frequented the Paris cafés when Hugo was there, a minor figure in the background. Ehrenburg was a force of nature, astoundingly prolific as a writer and propagandist, so successful and authoritative that Stalin's murderous assaults on his political rivals did not touch him, even as his close friend, Bukharin, was done in.

Ehrenburg needed an assistant who was fluent in German. Hugo had the right skills. Not that Ehrenburg was going to treat Hugo in a friendly way. He did not seem to remember him from the heady days in the Montparnasse cafés. He was curt with him. And later, when the war was over, he would barely register his presence. But at the moment, he needed someone like Hugo, a reliable Party member who was a native speaker of German and who was familiar with life in Germany and Austria.

Ehrenburg, who was fluent in French, did not know German and hated the Germans. Hugo was now expected to read a mass of captured materials, letters from family members in Germany sent to their sons and husbands at the front, and also, among other things, letters meant to be posted that had come to rest in the pockets of dead or captured soldiers. Hugo chose particularly striking items and translated them for Ehrenburg, who could now dig into these most intimate expressions of fear, of doom, of rage against the Hitler regime and its wars and use these authentic artifacts to attack the fading morale of the hated enemy.

That summer of 1944 was when German armies were at last in full retreat. In the west, Rome had been liberated and the American and British armies had landed in Normandy. On the Russian front, the bitter conflict, which had already cost the lives of millions, would soon end as a hard-fought victory for the Soviet forces, strengthened with American matériel and steadily resupplied with armor and airplanes from the Soviet industrial complexes in the East, beyond the reach of German bombers.

Working for Ehrenburg, Hugo accompanied him several times, heading by air to different army groups, but it was winter, that ice-cold winter of 1944, before Hugo received his own marching orders. He was to accompany a platoon of twenty-eight Austrian prisoners who had graduated from Leo Stern's political reeducation camp. A Red Army captain, Adrian Kristoforski, was on hand as the military commander of the newly formed unit, and Hugo was to act as its political commissar. For the first and last time, Hugo was headed for the front. He had hardly, before now, been in real danger in the course of more than three years of savage, total war—not since the first day, anyway, that day in June 1941 in Lwów, when the German offensive began.

While the Douglas DC-3, a lend-lease offering to the Soviet war effort, was warming up on the tarmac, Hugo slipped on his new uniform. The twenty-eight Austrian prisoners were also issued brand-new Red Army uniforms. At five in the morning they took off and headed for Bucharest, where they were forced to wait almost a week while the right engine was repaired. Taking off again, they flew along the Danube valley until they were suddenly approached by two Messerschmidt fighters. The slow-moving DC-3 was an easy target for the German attack planes. Preparing for the worst, the passengers stared at the cloud formations their pilot managed to slip in and out of until he lost the Messerschmidts at last, over the Hungarian city of Arad, where he put down and rolled across the snow-covered military airfield.

Hugo, leading his troop of ex-prisoners, now in Red Army uniforms, followed military convoys along half-destroyed roads and bridges, amid snow storms and the burning remains of what had just recently been heavy combat. As anyone familiar with military life would understand, fast-moving engagements are typically followed by endless waiting. Under orders to stop in a badly shot up small Hungarian market town, Hugo's troop hunkered down in Szolnok, where the Russian artillery batteries had been located before they moved on in the direction of Budapest. There was not much to see other than white farmhouses set in the snow.

While waiting for orders to keep moving, they requisitioned a large inn that had served as the headquarters of the Hungarian fascist commander. In the courtyard, the men started roasting sheep over open fires. In the gypsy tavern adjacent to the inn, wine flowed from barrels. Engineer units threw a pontoon bridge over the river and dealt as best they could with the burning town hall and grain silo. News from the front was encouraging: the Germans were in full retreat. When Hugo and a platoon of his men moved on, in the midst of a minor snow storm, toward Jász-Apáti (today Jászapáti), the next stage of their progression in the direction of Budapest, they encountered Marshall Malinowski, the commanding officer of the Third Ukrainian Army Corps, calmly riding a horse. They had to move out of the way to let him pass, together with his entourage. There was now a lengthy stay in the village of Apati, which appeared inhabited exclusively by women, children, and old men, since men of military age had been removed by the Germans.

When the time came to move again, Hugo rode in the special propaganda truck equipped with loudspeakers. In the distance, the sounds of artillery fire could be heard as they came closer to Budapest. From a close suburb of the capital city, they watched the battle for Budapest unfold. The Red Army already controlled the city in large part, but up at the royal castle of Buda, SS units were still holding out, hoping for the arrival of relief columns that never materialized. The city was encircled by Soviet forces. No relief columns could have saved the four divisions of Waffen SS under General Wildenbruch's command. The general surrendered at last. He was interrogated by Hugo's colleague, Major Wilmont.

As it happens, I was in Budapest at the time, a ten-year-old boy in hiding. Of course, I did not know that Hugo Huppert was in town and he knew nothing about me. My own experience of the battle of Budapest, in January and February 1945, was naturally different from Hugo's, except that we were both deafened by the wild roar of the Soviet guns and rockets. Being on the receiving end, to be sure, was not the same as riding in loudspeaker-equipped trucks behind the front lines. One thing that struck me as I read Hugo's account of his progress toward the battle zone was the image of Marshall Malinowski on horseback, in the snow, an image hard to reconcile with one's idea of modern warfare. But I do not doubt that Hugo saw the officer riding past. As it happens I, too, have a memory of Soviet military men riding past, swiftly, through the snow-covered street, as I opened the heavy door to the building where I had found refuge. This is what I remembered, the vision of the liberation of Budapest that I carried in my memory all those years, but I could not quite believe it. A mirage? A ten-year-old boy's imagination? No. At last I know that there really were Red Army scouts on horseback that day. Hugo confirms it.

While the Waffen SS divisions dug in along the hills of Buda were still holding out, Hugo's propaganda troop was sending out calls for surrender, round the clock, in German, from their batteries of loudspeakers set up along the Danube across from Buda. It was a very dangerous position.

One of his men was killed by the occasional machine-gun fire coming from the enemy positions, high up on the other side of the river.

In the city itself, in Pest, the civilian population had suffered throughout the siege, hungry and cold, surrounded by frozen corpses. Hugo's unit, the Seventh Command—the propaganda unit attached to the Army Group—took over an elegant mansion, a rare, luxurious refuge in the midst of the chaos and heartbreak of war. Here Hugo spent time with Major Mischa Kwesselava, with whom he had become friendly during their stay in the village of Jász-Apáti. Mischa was a philologist from Tbilisi. Hugo, characteristically, found solace in the arms of a young woman whom he describes as unhappily married and begging him to take her away. Her name was Etty.

Past conquered Budapest, the victorious armies moved ever closer to Vienna and the end of the war, as winter gave way to early spring. Hugo, together with other Austrian and German Communists in Red Army uniforms, was beginning to feel his years of exile coming to an end. This was something he had been wishing for all along. Just what would await him upon his return to Vienna, not to mention Bielitz, was impossible to imagine, except that he knew that his entire past in the cities of his youth would have been erased. He would not be coming home to anyone. He would merely find familiar places, eroded by bombs and fires, and empty of the people he once knew and loved.

On a freezing morning in early March, Hugo crossed into Austrian territory, as he puts it, "without a passport, without luggage," wearing the uniform of the Red Army, a pistol at his side. His orders were to win over the local population and to instruct Marshall Tolbukhin's staff about the intricacies of Austrian political realities. Moving into one village after another, the propaganda unit encountered hostile farming families, mostly women, children, and wounded soldiers sent back from the front and old men. In one farmstead they discovered a gruesome sight. In an underground wine cellar, they found an entire extended family, including nursing mothers, lying on mattresses neatly lined up against the walls, all dead and frozen. Apparently they had decided to commit mass suicide, believing that the approaching Russians would rape the women and kill everyone. A little farther down the road, a dead woman was hanging from a tree. She, too, had committed suicide out of fear, having been told by the local Nazi Party boss that the Russians would do terrible things to the women.

Understandably, Hugo was torn between the long-anticipated homecoming, after so many years of exile, and his fear of finding his return sullied by years of Nazi indoctrination and weighed down by the terrible losses Hitler's war had inflicted on everyone. Now that Marshall Tolbukhin's Third Ukrainian Army Group was no more than ten kilometers from Vienna's outer suburbs, crossing the plain of Wagram, where Napoleon had defeated the Austrians in 1809, Hugo understood that the city risked being totally demolished. On April 6, the Soviet forces completed the encirclement of the city. Armored units of the Red Army were reaching the banks of the Danube and turning toward the inner city while the Germans were getting ready to blow up public buildings and major infrastructure, including the bridges over the Danube. Instead of surrendering, Nazi formations engaged in suicidal attacks and continued to seek out and kill opponents.

As Hugo came closer to the center of the city, now largely abandoned by the enemy, he drove past burning ruins in an American-made Jeep. There were no people to be seen. His spirits sank. At the very moment when he would have been expected to cry out in triumph, he knew he was in the grip of a deep depression. What went through his mind now, as he skirted obstacles along the highway empty of traffic and people, was that he should not have left the comfort of his Russian family and of the country that had welcomed him, only to land in this seemingly familiar landscape: I no longer belong here, he kept saying to himself. But the very stones spoke to him. He understood the language of the walls.

"So there you are, my damned, treacherous Vienna," he muttered to himself as they were driving past the Belvedere Gardens and coming to a stop in the middle of Schwarzenberg square. Farther, in the very heart of the burning city, the Stephansplatz appeared as a dark mass of ruins. Along soot-covered walls, posters still ordered "fighting right up to the last cobblestone." Meanwhile, the SS commander had already made a discreet exit and small groups of local resistance fighters were making contact with the Soviet command. Several German officers who had helped the local resistance groups were caught by the Gestapo and executed. Their bodies were hanging from lamp posts. Most of the bridges had been destroyed by the retreating German units.

Vienna was now liberated. Hugo saw himself as unattached, free as a bird, lacking family, lacking relatives, owning nothing, having no secure roof over his head. He was back: this was really his town, and yet it was foreign. Returning at last from a very long exile, he felt both triumphant and deeply saddened. He pulled himself together, facing the innumerable tasks that needed to be taken on, quickly. Weeks would go by, endless meetings, much work. Bringing order to the country was not an overnight task.

A particularly significant meeting took place by candlelight in an apartment at Kantgasse Number 3. Hugo was there, representing the political department of the Army Corps. The meeting was chaired by Johann Koplenig, who had just arrived on a flight from Moscow. Koplenig was a genuine worker and an early adherent to the Austrian Communist Party. He had been captured by the Russians during the First World War. As a prisoner of war, he joined the Bolshevik Party and became active as a political speaker in German and Austrian prisoner of war camps in the Ural region. In a way, he was doing what Hugo would do some twenty years later. After serving in a number of important political positions in the Party, he took refuge in the Soviet Union. His wife, Hilde Oppenheim, the daughter of an astronomer, was a historian.

Koplenig led the all-night discussion about the future of the new Austrian Republic. At the head of the newly reconstituted state would be Karl Renner, the Social Democrat who had served as chancellor of the first republic. He would be assisted and advised by a three-person board of which Koplenig would be a member. Communists returning from exile would dominate the new government. Comrade Huppert observed the proceedings without claiming a political role. He was present as a representative of the Soviet-controlled press office which was about to establish two German-language newspapers, replacing the now defunct Nazi papers. One paper, the *Österreichische Zeitung*, was to be the voice of the Soviet occupation forces. The other, *Neues Österreich*, would be run by Ernst Fischer, one of the returning Hotel Lux Comintern operatives who would be appointed to the post of minister of culture.

Comrade Huppert, still a Red Army major, took over the cultural pages of the *Österreichische Zeitung*.

Vienna was now divided into four separate occupation zones: Russian, American, British, and French. Hugo took up residence in a modern apartment building in the Russian zone, across from the Palais Coburg, in the city center. In those early days, the city lacked streetcars, buses, bridges, and a functioning telephone network. To lift the spirits of the traumatized population, Hugo's unit was ordered to organize popular festivities in celebration of Labor Day (May 1, everywhere except in the United States). The sun was shining that day in the park he had chosen for the event, while distant artillery fire could still be heard. A few days later, on May 9, the war in Europe was over. (I remember the church bells ringing wildly that day, near a Slovak meadow where I was herding geese.) The new Austrian Republic was being proclaimed, with flags flying and martial music.

Hugo, as he remembers the event, turned to a macabre accounting of the war just completed: 380,000 Austrian citizens died in Hitler's wars, 12,622 Viennese men, women, and children were killed in bombing raids, 185,426 of Hugo's fellow citizens died in Hitler's concentration camps, mostly Jews but also Communists and Socialists. Among the dead whom he does not mention are his own dead, including his brother Josef and just about anyone he knew in Bielitz. Aside from his brother, for whose fate he feels responsible, he does not dwell on the large cohort of relatives, friends, and acquaintances lost in the war years. His Parisian uncle, Emmanuel, died of natural causes, but what happened to his cheerful Aunt Paula? And what about the Reich sons he had known in Paris and the Reich relatives back in Polish or Ukrainian towns? Uncle Vinzenz, the railway engineer, whom he saw briefly for the last time in Lwów in June 1941? Surprisingly, Margit Reich, the artist, who had also been in Lwów that day, resurfaced after the war in a letter preserved in his archive.

Hugo was too busy, working too hard, to entertain melancholy thoughts. He worked at the newspaper while also acting as Marshall Konjev's personal translator. His depression retreated momentarily, especially when he discovered that Julianne Artbauer, Emily's mother, was alive. He rushed over to her place and hugged her. They had much to say to each other. She lived alone now. She was the only living human being from his past to whom Hugo could claim to be returning.

Instead of evoking the ghosts of his past, Hugo eventually entered into one of the most fruitful and worry-free periods of his life. Here he was, at home in Vienna, after all those years of exile and deprivation, a Soviet officer of the occupation force, with all sorts of special privileges, including the most comfortable living quarters he had ever had. In spite of the immense difficulties facing the city's leaders, in spite of the ruined buildings and the rubble in the streets, this first spring since the elimination of the Nazi enemy was full of hope.

There was music! As early as April 27, there was a performance of Mozart's *The Marriage of Figaro* at the Volksoper, under the direction of Josef Krips, returned from exile. The election of Theodor Körner—who had been a general in the Austrian army in the First World War and who joined the Social Democratic Party in the postwar years, and who was imprisoned both by the right-wing Dollfuss regime and the Nazis—to the post of Vienna's mayor was another instance of the return of one of Hitler's victims to power. Körner would eventually be elected to the country's presidency. Hugo had occasional contacts with the mayor, but he maintained a sustained relationship with Victor Matejka, who was in charge of the city's cultural affairs. Matejka had been an inmate of the Dachau concentration camp. He was, according to Hugo, an essential figure in the reconstruction of Vienna's cultural life, promoting artists and musicians and financing improvised theatrical venues to make up for those, including the Burgtheater, that had been heavily damaged.

In his personal life, if his explanations can be trusted, Hugo moved heaven and earth to try and persuade his wife to join him in Vienna, together with twelve-year-old Annette, but to no avail. Once again, he felt his depression returning. He may have given the idea of a return to Moscow some thought, but in reality his Viennese life was too enjoyable to consider giving it up. Especially now. He had just very recently, by chance, run into a girl he had seen two years earlier at the home of an acquaintance, Commissar Shurbin. She was twenty years old at the time and very pretty. When he dined at the Shurbins, he never could take his eyes off her. She took care of the Shurbin children, she helped with dinner, she sat at the table with the family and guests, joining the conversation, speaking German with a Hungarian accent. Who was this girl?

He may not have known much about her at the time, but now, in September 1947, she stood before him in the waiting room of the Soviet offices where he had business and she appeared distraught. What is the matter, Maria, he asked? Maria, whom he remembered as the lively girl at the Shurbins' dinner table, now appeared despondent. Dear Doctor Huppert, she began to explain: the Shurbin family left, suddenly, when Commissar Shurbin was sent to Bucharest and was not allowed to take Maria with him, as this would have been completely forbidden by the occupation forces' regulations. Maria had no papers. She was a "Displaced Person."

Now twenty-two, Maria had no way of making a living. She was alone in Vienna. Could not Doctor Huppert, with his many connections, help her? Doctor Huppert, as one can easily imagine, was overcome with emotion—and desire. To be sure, the old Doctor Huppert, many years later, when he sat at his desk and described his relationship with Maria, would deny having had unworthy thoughts as the young woman pleaded with him for help in that waiting room, back in September 1947.

But here is what happened, according to his recollections. He felt a wave of sympathy for her. He remembered how powerfully he had been affected by her at the Shurbins' dinner table. He wanted to help her and he was in the position to do so, still a Red Army major and a well-known figure around town. There was no time to find a family that might replace the Shurbins and employ Maria, providing her with room and board. No, the girl was in a desperate spot, she had been crying, she needed help right away, and there was no time to waste. And so Hugo took what would eventually prove to be a fateful decision: he would step in himself to provide for her. He offered to take her on as a part-time housekeeper the very next day. His kindness had an immediate effect on the girl: she bent to kiss his hand. Hugo stopped her just in time, and was moved to touch her under her chin, delicately, as one would with a child.

With that instinctive gesture, Hugo began a dangerous relationship with Maria. In his memoirs he devotes some eighty pages to what he calls "the history of a mistake." In those pages he also professes innocence. He had no intention of taking advantage of the desirable woman begging for his help. He was just doing the decent thing. And Maria, he makes clear, was a truly remarkable person who found herself in a desperate situation through no fault of her own. Hugo makes it clear that he was fully aware of the dangers of the situation.

What would, under other circumstances, have been a totally innocuous matter—the hiring of an adult servant who might at some point grace her employer's bed—was in occupied Vienna something different and dangerous. Had Hugo reverted to being an Austrian citizen, there would have been no problem at all. But as a Soviet citizen, as a Party member, and, above all, as an officer of the Red Army, he was subject to very clear rules that did not permit intimate relations with the local population. This explains Hugo's lengthy protestations of innocence in the affair. He hired Maria to help her, nothing else. She was to do his housekeeping from nine to one daily and he would be at work during those hours, so there would be no contact with the bewitching Maria. Shortly after she began her duties, Hugo was called away to Moscow as part of a delegation to join in the celebrations around the thirtieth anniversary of the October Revolution. Maria was charged with keeping the household functioning in Hugo's absence. And why not move into the comfortable apartment while he was away?

While in Moscow, he took the opportunity to spend a few hours with Vera and Annette, pleading with Vera, asking her to consider joining him in Vienna. She made it clear that she had no intention of leaving for what she viewed as enemy territory. She would not raise Annette in a foreign country. That was that.

Returning to Vienna, he had to admit the obvious: he no longer had a family, since he had no intention of returning to the Soviet Union. He was at home in Austria. And in his well-kept apartment on the Heumühlgasse, there was young Maria, waiting for his return. His arrival in Vienna, on a snowy evening with poor visibility, was solidly anchored in his memory: he saw Maria's graceful figure in the distance, her threadbare winter coat. She came toward him at the corner of the Heumühlgasse and the Kettenbrückengasse, her eyes filled with tears of joy. He resisted a natural impulse to embrace her in public, because he was fully aware of the drastic regulations governing intimate contact between the Soviet military and the Austrian population.

But things were changing now in Hugo's daily life: he was working at home, sitting at his desk, while Maria carried on with her cleaning and cooking, He now had his lunch with her, in the kitchen. He was in the habit of handing Maria free tickets to a movie theater, one of the perks available to him as the theater critic of the *Österreichische Zeitung*. And then, one fateful evening, returning from work, he saw that Maria had gone to see the film for which he had given her a free pass. Driven by the kind of feverish excitement that must have usually accompanied his practiced moves, Hugo turned on his heel and headed for the movie theater where he knew he would find Maria.

As he recalls that evening, he offers the reader a heartfelt remembrance of his approach, his method for seducing young women. He found his way to the row in the darkened theater where Maria was sitting. He took the seat next to hers, touching her shoulder and thigh in the process. He grasped her arm and whispered in her ear, explaining that he just now decided he wanted to see the film. The girl's scent and her warm body had an undeniable effect on Hugo. All at once, Maria was no longer his housekeeper: his relationship with the girl sitting at his side had moved to another level. The darkened theater now struck him as an overcrowded waiting room. He could barely wait for the lights to come on.

Would Maria get angry at him? He was angry at himself and ashamed. But he could not resist the powerful impulse that was driving him headlong toward a situation he would not be able to control. Ashamed? Certainly. Was he not about to take advantage of the poor girl? What was she thinking? Perhaps, even most likely, she was offended as he took her arm. Could she resist him when a refusal might lead to utter, helpless destitution? In spite of her pretty face, in spite of her friendly laughter, she was entirely vulnerable, with nowhere to go and no papers. She was a Displaced Person—and he was her employer.

She was quiet. Did she feel cornered? He took her to a café on the Mariahilferstrasse where they had something to eat and drank some Riesling. Around midnight, he accompanied her to her friend's apartment where she had been sleeping, and now, suddenly, he said to her: "If you like, but only if you really want to." He was needy. His dearest people, as he put it, were gone. He needed to be loved. Perhaps she, too, felt such a need. "Only if you yourself really want to, only if you are entirely sure," he kept saying, as he proposed moving her into the spare bedroom of his apartment.

"I don't know, I am afraid," she said. He kept thinking about the drastic wording of the regulations affecting "commerce with the local population." He is himself, of course, as local as one can be, but he had not yet relinquished his Soviet citizenship and his army rank. Finally Maria said to him: "Look, Doctor Huppert, allow me to take two days to go see my sister. I will follow her advice."

While Maria was away, Hugo consulted with his friend, Captain Axelrod. Those in the know were aware that Axelrod lived with his local girlfriend, Uschi. The Soviet captain's advice was clear and urgent: whatever you do, keep it completely to yourself. Do not advertise your relationship. Do not tell ANYONE!

Two days later, when Maria was slated to return from visiting her sister, Lisa, Hugo met the train and watched Maria pull a backpack out of the compartment, laughing all the while. "Where are you taking this thing?" he asked. To the Heumühlgasse, she answered. That was that. She moved in. Hugo had placed a bouquet of roses in her room. "Here you are at home," he said to her. They fell into each other's arms. Those tender embraces, writes Hugo many years later, were a refuge from the cold and fears of the war years.

Well and good. To what extent can the reader trust Hugo's account? It is "poetic reportage" and, at the same time, obviously, an attempt to justify his behavior. What was Maria thinking? Yes, she was an adult, but she was dependent on her employer's good will. Was Hugo taking advantage of her? One suspects that he was, indeed. Why does he go on at such great length describing his affair with Maria? That is something we will soon understand. That this was an especially meaningful relationship is clear, even though he strayed twice, while he was living with Maria, according to his own account, with women about whom he says almost nothing.

It is understandable that Hugo, having just lost his Russian family and feeling sorry for himself, with the threat of depression on the way, would cling to the pretty twenty-two-year-old. It would be pointless to ask whether Maria remembered that evening at the movies and what followed differently from Hugo's account. He presents a fairly thick and convincing dossier about Maria. She and her sister, four years older, were the daughters of a farming family near the small town of Nagy Kikinda in Yugoslavia. Their father was no longer alive. The mother somehow was gone. The girls were displaced by the war. Maria had worked for the Shurbin family, while Lisa found a place in the Austrian countryside, cooking for the village priest.

Hugo, in his seventies, remembers Maria with deep feeling as an innocent being. He was hopelessly in love with her. He felt that his union with Maria was almost a marriage, notwithstanding that he had not divorced Vera and continued to hope she would change her mind and join him in Vienna. Maria knew about Vera, although Vera did not know about Maria. Maria, like everyone in Vienna, was perfectly aware of the rigid rules that forbade intimate relations between the Soviet military and the local population.

Both Hugo and Maria were looking forward to the end of the occupation and the resumption of normal life in Austria when their living together would become acceptable. In the meantime, Hugo was happier than he had ever been. In the course of his infatuation with Maria, who was young and strikingly attractive, Hugo went out of his way to display her in public. He bought expensive clothes for her. Dressed like a princess, he tells us, she accompanied him everywhere. The couple showed up at diplomatic receptions, at the Opera, at concerts. And all the while, Hugo was fully aware of the fact that he was courting disaster. He was warned by friends and even by Russian officers to whom he reported. Somehow, wearing civilian clothes and feeling at home in his Vienna, he seems to have pushed reality away.

On February 15, 1949, everything came to an abrupt end. At 5 PM a sergeant showed up at his office and informed him that he was wanted, urgently, at headquarters. After being driven in an open jeep in a nasty snow storm, he reported to the commanding officer. Told he was scheduled to return to Moscow immediately, he understood that the reckoning was at hand. He was not allowed to leave the headquarters building and was quickly ushered into the waiting DC-9 transport plane, under guard. Once again, for the first time since his arrest in 1938, the poet and journalist Hugo Huppert found himself tossed about, helplessly, by forces beyond his control.

CHAPTER-SEVEN

HOURS LATER, THE FEAR WAS SINKING IN. AFTER A PERILOUS takeoff from the snow-covered field, Hugo began considering his future. Prison? Siberia? Those four years of freedom in Vienna now began to feel like a momentary escape from life in Stalin's world. He had been giddy with the coming of peace and had felt at home at last in his old Vienna, in spite of the ruined buildings and the tattered feel of the exhausted city. Moving through the well-known streets as a member of the occupying military, settled in an apartment luxurious beyond belief from the perspective of someone who had never in his adult life lived in anything other than cramped, shared lodgings, Hugo must have forgotten that he was not, after all, free to do as he wished.

Inviting Maria into his household, exhibiting her at public functions, he had thrown caution to the wind, acting like a free man when he was, in fact, a Soviet citizen, a member of the Communist Party and an officer of the Red Army. If only, he wrote years later, he had given up his Soviet citizenship, resigned his commission, and become an Austrian citizen again.

On arrival in Moscow, he was taken to the office of General Burzew, who was commanding the political division of the Red Army. Burzew knew him slightly. During the war years he had worked with prominent German Communists, including Erich Weinert and Alfred Kurella. He received Hugo in a jovial manner, allowing him to phone Vera. Hugo was free to go to their apartment.

When the door opened, his daughter, Annette, already sixteen years old, greeted him exuberantly. Looking at his wife, he wondered whether he was welcome. Later, when they were alone, Vera made her position clear: she did not care about Maria. She just wanted to know what he was doing in Moscow and how long he expected to stay. He told her the truth: this was not another official trip. He had been recalled, most likely because of his relationship with Maria. The fact that Maria came from Yugoslavia, at the very time of Stalin's assault on Tito's "treason," no doubt had much to do with Hugo's immediate recall. He did not know what would happen to him.

Vera made it clear that he was no longer welcome in her bedroom and he was not to eat his meals in his wife's and daughter's company. She treated him as someone who was dangerous, someone whose as yet unknown fate could prove contagious. For some time nothing happened. Hugo arranged to do translation work. Eventually the day of reckoning was at hand. He was called in front of the Central Commission for Review and Purge of the Party's ranks. He appeared before Comrade Shkiriatov, an old Bolshevik who chaired the commission. Accusing Hugo of inexcusable negligence, of relations with suspicious persons, Shkiriatov threw Hugo's Party membership booklet into a drawer.

That was it: he was excluded. He felt degraded. As for Vera, she immediately concluded that only divorce had a chance of protecting her and her daughter. Two weeks later it was done. No longer a member of the Party, he was now no longer a husband. He was on his way to being a non-person. He wandered the city's streets aimlessly, stopped shaving, and sank into a deep depression, feeling as helpless as he had after Emily's sudden death. He could see no way out of his predicament. As a Soviet citizen he could not leave the country without permission, and as someone now excluded from Party membership, he had no hope of returning to Vienna, to his girl, Maria, to his Viennese friends, and to the comfortable life he had enjoyed there. In Moscow he now had no family, no place to live, and only a bare minimum income from translations.

At this absolute low point in his life, a call came through for him from the Writers' Union offices. The secretary asked him to stop by. When he did, as soon as the door opened, he saw, to his amazement, his old army friend Mischa, who greeted him effusively. Mischa was wearing civilian clothes. They had last seen each other in liberated Vienna, four years earlier. Now Mischa was back in his native Georgian home in Tbilisi. A civilian now, he was president of the Georgian Society for Cultural Relations with Foreign Countries. And he had a proposition for Hugo: he was looking for someone who could translate the Georgian national epic, attributed to the medieval poet Rustaveli, into German.

The chief administrator of the Writers' Union, Alexander Fadeyev, knew Hugo's successful German versions of Mayakovsky's poetry, and he had gotten together with Mischa to suggest the Rustaveli commission, perhaps as a way of rescuing Hugo from his current predicament. Still, even though the task seemed almost impossible (1,671 four-line strophes in a language Hugo did not know), there were several capable Russian versions of the poem, some in manuscript, housed in the Georgian Academy of the Arts in Tbilisi. What Mischa had in mind was to bring Hugo to Tbilisi to get started on the work.

Hugo turned for advice to a hugely influential woman, Jelena Stassowa, an old Communist worthy who knew him and knew his situation. She advised him to accept Mischa's offer and, at the same time, to set petitions in motion to overturn his exclusion from the Party. This would be a slow process requiring affidavits from powerful people, including Stassowa herself, as well as Helmut Liebknecht, who was back in Moscow. Encouraged by Stassowa, Hugo began to feel his depression lifting. He felt the pull of the warm south, that land of steep mountains, of orchards and vineyards, of roses, oleander, and cypresses. He suddenly realized that the Rustaveli commission, however fraught with difficulty, was about to rescue him from his sad and fearful life in Moscow. He took Stassowa's advice, collected affidavits, and arranged travel to Georgia.

In Tbilisi, the capital city, he stayed at first with his friend Mischa (Lenin Street 63) and eventually would live in various apartments and hotels while making contact with a number of eminent literary figures. He received a generous salary, downright princely when compared to his measly earnings for occasional translations in Moscow. Although the task facing him was certainly daunting, the appeal of a temporary residence in Georgia was undeniable. It was a way of exchanging his drab and anxious life in Moscow for a new life in the south, meeting new people, shedding his ex-prisoner outlook and his fear of being arrested once again. The political atmosphere in Moscow, just then, was poisoned by a campaign against "cosmopolitan" writers. Writers Hugo knew were being denounced right and left. Moscow was not a safe place for someone as "cosmopolitan" as Hugo, someone who had been excluded from the Party and had served prison time.

Not that there was any real possibility of evading the scrutiny of the secret police wherever you were in the Soviet world. But Hugo could not help hanging on to a scrap of hope, hope for a return to freedom and to his Viennese life. Mischa had suggested such a hopeful outcome: produce a German version of Rustaveli's epic, *The Knight in the Tiger Skin*, and Stalin would be enchanted! He was a Georgian, after all, and known as a fanatic lover of Rustaveli's poem. Who knows, perhaps that would suffice to restore Comrade Huppert to his rights and allow him to return to Vienna.

Alternating between resignation and hope, Hugo had left behind his heady Viennese days, when everything seemed possible, when there was no need to submit, to calculate what was permissible. From the moment when he was ordered to board the plane that would take him to Moscow, he became, once again, Soviet Man, resigned to his powerlessness, to being at the mercy of cruel and arbitrary forces. Writing in the 1970s, long after Stalin's death, Hugo managed to resurrect his down-trodden self from when he walked Moscow's winter streets back in 1950 and all seemed lost: Vienna, Europe, Maria, Vera, any sense of the future. Only one thing now provided at least an illusion of a life ahead: Georgia!

Clinging to the notion that Stalin, the all-powerful Father (*der Väterliche*), would show mercy and offer forgiveness (*Gnade*) for Hugo's transgressions, once his version of the beloved Georgian national epic reached his desk, Hugo threw himself into the impossible task. His life was at stake, he believed. He would labor, month after month, in hotel rooms in Tbilisi, in Moscow libraries, in various scenic vacation spots provided by his sponsors, and complete the task on time.

The Georgian venture turned out to be a success in the long run, not because Stalin would pardon the poet—he would soon die anyway—but because it served to lift Hugo's spirits and allowed him to make good use of his chief talent. His astonishing facility with languages had allowed him to present Mayakovsky's poetry in German-language versions that were much more than translations. They were *Nachdichtungen*, poems in their own right, coming as close as possible to the original but reimagined in a poetic language anchored in another culture, with its own poetic traditions. Robert Lowell's version of Racine's *Phèdre* is a good example of this special art of which Hugo was becoming a master.

As a sample of Hugo's exceptional rhymed version of *The Knight in the Tiger Skin*, here is a typical quatrain rendered in German:

Wie die Sonne gleiche Lichtflut auf Untat und Rosen giesst,
sieh, dass Arm' und Reich du mit gleicher Fürstengnade misst.
Auch den Trotz bezwing durch Güte, die allzeit bezwingend ist;
spende—wie die Flut, vom vollen Meere kommend, meerwarts fliesst.

Creating medieval German poetry out of 1,671 quatrains originally preserved in Georgian oral tradition and helpfully translated into several Russian versions would have seemed simply impossible to most translators, particularly when faced with a deadline for delivery at hand. Among those who turned Mischa down, there was, it seems, another German Communist émigré whom Hugo knew quite well, Alfred Kurella, an experienced writer and translator. Although several years his senior, Kurella's biography resembled Hugo's, except that he had been active as a Party functionary. A Soviet citizen since 1937, Kurella experienced the usual tragic realities of Soviet life under Stalin. His brother, Heinrich, was arrested by the NKVD and executed. This did not prevent Alfred from continuing his Soviet propaganda work, both in Russia and, after 1954, in East Germany. That kind of quiet acceptance of murderous injustices was the hallmark of those years.

When Hugo arrived in Georgia in August 1950, he was once again taken under the wing of a powerful older woman. As in Moscow, where Lilya Brik had smoothed the way for him, where Stassowa advised him and interceded for him, he found support from another influential older woman, the writer and translator Fatma Twaltwadse. She knew everyone in the closed world of the Georgian intelligentsia. Through her good offices he found himself invited to live in the home of Nina Tabidze, the widow of Tizian Tabidze, one of the country's most honored poets: he, too, like Kurella's brother and so many others, had been arrested and executed in 1937. His widow, Nina, like so many survivors, just went on with her life, not allowing her suffering to show.

Hugo spent twenty-eight months, without respite, translating Rustaveli's epic, polishing those verses and infusing them with life. He traveled across the Georgian countryside, notebook in hand, to record landscapes and ruins, authentic remains of the twelfth-century world depicted in Rustaveli's poem. He went so far as to give Rustaveli's heroine, the Princess Nestan-Daredshan, something of the traits of his current lover, who shared a hotel room with him in Tbilisi when he was not Nina Tabidze's lodger. In this way, one might say, he succeeded in combining his two chief talents, the mastery of words and the seduction of women.

This is as good a place as any to note that Hugo was not universally liked. Beginning with his father, whose letters in the 1920s duly noted his faults, there is a long list of people who could not stand him, including powerful figures in the émigré community, such as his boss in Moscow, the novelist and poet Johannes Becher, who later became the minister of culture in the DDR. (In his published memoir, Hugo is respectful and friendly toward Becher. In private conversation with an American researcher, late in life and with Becher dead, however, he referred to him simply as a "swine.")

Hugo maintained life-long friendships with a number of men—to say nothing of the legions of women—who appreciated his qualities. They tended to be German-speaking, often Jewish, literary people with musical interests, in other words, people with whom he had a great deal in common. Some were older and famous, like Egon Erwin Kisch, whom Hugo admired and imitated in his reportages.

Kisch was Prague Jewish and a man of action. He started out writing feuilleton sketches for the Prague paper *Bohemia* in the early years of the century. He served in the Austrian military during the First World War and became a radical Communist. He wrote at least thirty books, fought in the Spanish Civil War, lived in exile in Mexico, and returned home after 1945. Hugo had met him years earlier in Berlin and learned a great deal from the experienced writer. Hugo's first book, the Siberian one, is clearly influenced by Kisch's entertaining way of luring the reader into his own worldview.

Hugo visited the old man in Prague after the war and wrote a thoughtful preface to an anthology of Kisch's writings published in Vienna in 1948. This was at the time of his stay in liberated and Russian-occupied Vienna. Those years may well have been the best years of Hugo's life, filled with both old and new friendships. In postwar Vienna, he may have found it easier, for the first time, to see himself as a happy and successful writer, instead of constantly feeling diminished when compared to towering figures in his Moscow exile, men like Ehrenburg or Becher, to whom he was expected to defer and who had power over him.

In Georgia, in the early 1950s, Hugo did not need to fear being overshadowed by eminent émigré writers: he was the only specimen of his kind in this land of orchards, vineyards, and picturesque ruins. There was a thriving literary culture, a Georgian culture, aristocratic still, and full of admiration for poetry. Rustaveli was the national poet, his name enshrined in street signs. Even though Hugo was so much better off in Georgia, free of the poisonous machinations of émigré eminences, he was also alone and he suffered from the absence of friends and family. He was incapable of remaining alone. He threw himself at women and occasionally needed psychiatric support. His diary entries acknowledge his need for support from the women he hastily fell in love with. They were almost therapeutic relationships. He makes this clear in letters to his father, as when he writes of his infatuation with Vera. He insists that he needs Vera in the way he needs water and air.

His closest relationship may well have been with his ever present diaries, his *Tagebücher*. Into their pages he poured his innermost thoughts. He admitted that he would rather write diary entries than anything else. He wrote this in the fall of 1931, in Moscow, still deeply disturbed in the aftermath of Emily's sudden death. Miluschka (his pet name for Emily) was his secret religion. Her influence over him, in those early years in Vienna, had been all-encompassing. He promised to follow the path she showed him. Miluschka accompanied him and showed him the way. Such private notations in the pages of his dear *Tagebücher* point to his utter dependence on Emily, who took charge of him when she was seventeen and who died at twenty-three. The language of these sad diary entries reminds one of something close to religious devotion. Emily was his goddess. He admitted he was not worthy of her.

Vera, too, was a goddess, except when things turned sour and Hugo, all at once, became filled with hatred for her. When she walked out on him, he was desperate. And then, when she returned he was deliriously happy all of a sudden. It is quite embarrassing to observe these hysterical mood swings of his, especially in Moscow in the 1930s. And those were surely trying years. He felt surrounded by enemies, by those published senior writers and politicians among the German-speaking émigrés who, he was convinced, looked down on him. When he triumphantly reported to his diary that he had just received his Soviet Communist Party card, number 1792910, on December 6, 1930, he noted: "My enemies are dumbfounded."

While there certainly were enemies, they were really, for the most part, senior figures exasperated by Hugo's behavior. Kurella, for instance, accused him of exaggerating the significance of his work and pointed to Hugo's vanity, which made him disliked all around. Again and again he found himself cast out by men he admired or with whom he had at first been on friendly terms, as in the case of Boris Pasternak or Willi Bredel. Becher, the editor-in-chief to whom he reported before his arrest in 1938, refused to rehire him when he was released. He told him to stop his constant resentments, *ressentiments*, echoing Papa Huppert, who used the word *Kränkungen* in a letter of 1922, meaning the same thing that Becher would complain about in 1939.

In Georgia, at last, he was not beholden to Party officials, not overshadowed by major figures in the émigré literary community. He was on his own, well paid, well lodged, in a land of absorbing, almost theatrical landscapes. Moscow was far away and he was well received in the homes of patrons such as Nina and Fatma. Of particular importance to him was the approbation of Professor Nubidze, an elderly academic who was tasked with evaluating Hugo's translation. Nubidze had been arrested, but he was eventually released on Stalin's orders.

When Hugo met him, Nubidze was an admired man about town, a womanizer, the owner of a vineyard, and a towering figure in the world of philology. Among other things, he had translated Rustaveli's poem into Russian. He was a man of the world, having studied in German universities in his youth. This was the man who was asked to judge Hugo's version on the basis of some 200 stanzas, offered as a sample. Hugo's versifying pleased the old man. He lived in his own villa in Tbilisi, Perowskaya number 6, a quiet street on the edge of town. There Hugo spent many an evening, listening to Nubidze's stories and profiting from his corrections to the evolving manuscript. In the background was Nubidze's wife, friendly, dressed in the latest Parisian fashion, bringing tea, fruit, and pastries.

In his published autobiography, Hugo devotes separate chapters to work and play in his Georgian exile. Work includes not only the relentless versifying, month after month, but also his sessions with Professor Nubidze and his frequent travels across the Georgian countryside. As an avid sightseer, he is drawn to the spectacular mountains and lakes of the region. He also makes a point of visiting the birthplace and childhood home of his hero, the late Vladimir Mayakovsky who grew up in the village of Baghdadi. Such outings may be seen, in some sense, as work related, as a systematic imbibing of local color. Even his frequent stays in luxurious resorts, paid for by GOKS, the sponsoring organization that monitored the progress of his work, can be understood as necessary to the timely completion of his contract.

The separate chapter describing play, as opposed to work, is largely an account of his many easy conquests of women. Hugo was in his fifties. Vera had divorced him. Maria, whom he worshipped, was lost to him. As an endangered specimen, no longer a Party member, constantly worried, unsure of his rights, he found himself quarantined, away from all contact with the world outside of the Soviet Union. In Tbilisi, which had become something of a tourist destination, Hugo was careful to avoid foreigners. He chose to stay in a hotel not frequented by tourists from western countries. In spite of his caution, he had some scares, even in out-of-the-way country resorts. In one instance he discovered that two unknown men were asking questions about him. He waited until evening and when darkness fell, he took off, running toward the local train station in a panic.

In Georgia, at least, he was far from Moscow and the intrigues among the émigrés. Thanks to his official position and to the patronage of Nubidze, of Fatma and Nina, he found himself appreciated and fêted, giving public readings and, generally, enjoying life in Georgia. His rehabilitation was moving along, slowly but surely, after Stalin's death in 1953. He began publishing in *Die Weltbühne*, an influential East German periodical in whose pages he would eventually become a regular and valued contributor. (On the occasion of his seventieth birthday, in 1972, he was interviewed by a *Weltbühne* colleague, Günter Caspar, who asked him whether he knew how many articles he had published in the weekly. Characteristically, Hugo answered: 322.)

Gradually, even before his rehabilitation, he had been preparing the ground for his return to Europe. He published a collection of poems with a Georgian theme (*Georgischer Wanderstab*, Berlin, 1954) and, finally, his German version of Rustaveli's *Knight in the Tiger Skin* (Berlin, 1955). The following year he was exonerated, at last. His Party membership was restored. He was now free to travel.

He received the final, very generous payments from GOKS. Exceptionally, he was allowed to bring some of the money with him when he was ready to leave the Soviet Union. The rest he handed over to Vera. Now came the packing up of the tools of his trade, the books and papers, the diaries, the letters: all this ended up filling eleven large packing cases, to be shipped to Vienna. At last he was ready to leave, having found time to say an emotional goodbye to the last of his Georgian girlfriends.

Now that he was a free man, he wrote to his editor in Berlin, Hans Leonard, and to old colleagues in Vienna, men like the journalist Bruno Frei, to announce his imminent arrival. It never occurred to Hugo that he could settle in any city but his Vienna, even though Vienna was now the capital of the newly autonomous Austrian Republic, no longer a ward of the Soviet occupation forces. Hugo's Vienna now belonged in the capitalist, "Imperialist" West. And here was Hugo Huppert, still a Soviet citizen, about to land in what some might describe as enemy territory. After a lifetime of absurd situations full of contradictions, this last one did not even warrant a moment's hesitation. He was going home.

It was a hard landing. At the Viennese airport, on April 4, 1956, Hugo was welcomed by Bruno Frei, whose wife, Elena, had left him years earlier. She had shared Frei's Mexican exile during the war years. Hugo had run into Elena in Moscow, and she had entrusted him with a letter to Bruno he was carrying in his coat pocket. Accompanying Bruno Frei was Steffi Zucker, representing her husband, the editor of the *Volkstimme* newspaper. The third member of the welcoming committee was a striking woman, none other than Hugo's Maria.

Hugo did not know what to say. He had heard from reliable sources that Maria, after his abrupt and unexplained departure, had found refuge with Ernst Fischer, whose wife, Ruth, had left him for a younger man. Fischer, now alone with his young daughter, needed someone to take charge of her. Maria moved in and in due course she found herself replacing Ruth. Fischer bought her luxurious clothes and jewelry and took her with him to concerts, openings, the theater.

Now, on that chilly April morning at the airport, there was the beautiful Maria, no longer a waif but a woman of thirty, *une femme de trente ans*, the woman of his dreams, the girl he had longed for in his Georgian exile. But she was no longer the same. He felt she was sullied by her association with Fischer, a man he hated and whom he suspected of having denounced him in 1938. He rode in Bruno Frei's car and quietly handed him Elena's letter. The man burst into tears and kissed the letter, overcome with emotion.

The little party headed for lunch at a hotel downtown. It was snowing. At the table, Hugo was seated across from Maria. It was clear to him that he was expected to talk things over with her. She might have thought that he would propose marriage. As he tells the story, more than twenty years later, in the very last pages of his autobiography, Hugo found himself bewildered by Maria's mature appearance. Where was the simple girl he had cherished all those years ago? The elegant woman in front of him, speaking an elegant German, was someone else. The Maria he had loved was dead for him.

Using such melodramatic words could not hide the reality. He was still deeply in love with her and as late as 1979, many years later, he showed his true feelings in a poem dedicated to her memory. He writes about those years when they lived together and remembers them as a true paradise. He adored everything about her. He remained bitter when he thought of the way in which they had been mercilessly separated. Although Maria eventually married someone else and had a little girl she called Elli, the old poet found himself regretting that he was not Elli's father.

Back in April 1956, when he was trying to settle in his old Vienna, his presumed relationship with Maria was only one of many thorny issues before him. Writing to Willi Bredel in September, he adopted a plaintive tone, telling him that he had no place to call his own, no reliable job, no family. Bredel, a fellow journalist and a member of the German Communist Party since 1919, had shared Hugo's Moscow exile and was now, together with most of the other German Communist political figures who had spent the war years in Moscow, settled in East Berlin.

Was there room for Hugo in Berlin? Bredel was skeptical. There is strong resistance to you here, he noted. Kurella, especially, was against him, as was Becher, who held the important post of minister of cultural affairs. Bert Brecht had backed him in the past, but he was gone. Perhaps no one wanted to see him in Berlin, but Hans Leonard, the editor of *Die Weltbühne*, clearly understood how useful Hugo Huppert could be as a clever polemicist and an outstanding reporter. Hugo would remain a regular contributor to Leonard's publication for many years to come. The Hungarian revolt of 1956 would offer an opportunity for Hugo to display his talents.

Right now, though, in April of that year, Hugo was trying to find his footing in the new Vienna, a city no longer Red and no longer under Soviet control. To begin with, he had to regain his Austrian citizenship, which took some doing and required the assistance of a lawyer. This settled, eventually, he had to assure his livelihood. Writing for *Die Weltbühne* made sense, as did other journalistic assignments. Translations and adaptations of Mayakovsky's poetry found a ready audience. And then there were the very successful travel articles he wrote initially for Leonard's *Weltbühne*, but which, soon enough, became part of a truly popular book under the title of *Münzen im Brunnen* (Coins in the Fountain).

That book, building on articles originally commissioned by Leonard, offered East German readers charming escapes into sunny Italian resort areas off-limits to them. Hugo became the genial host of these annual spring and summer excursions into the forbidden Western tourist paradises. While he himself was free to sample the pleasures of Italian cities on modest expense accounts, his readers, to be sure, could only follow him in their imagination, since they were marooned in their Stalinist world, behind barbed wire and even brick walls. The success of his book was due in no small part to the practiced skills of the feuilleton artist. Even though there is enough of more or less unobtrusive propaganda in those pages, they are a real pleasure to read.

Hugo would eventually manage to underwrite his Viennese life with royalties and subsidies (and possibly also stipends from the DDR security establishment, the STASI). None of this, I would imagine, was assured when he first arrived from Moscow. That dispiriting day in April, when he rejected a relationship with Maria, was followed, according to his own account, by a dramatic lunch meeting to which he had been invited by his old nemesis, the Communist politician Ernst Fischer.

Fischer's new wife, the formidable Lou, who had previously been married to the composer Hanns Eisler and who had just published a novel, was at the table—and so was Maria. Ostensibly, they were gathered to talk about Lou's book, but it soon became obvious that Hugo had been ambushed with the intention of facilitating a permanent reunion with Maria, who still lived with the Fischers and took care of Titi, Fischer's young daughter.

The lunch turned into a true disaster, as Hugo threw down his napkin and responded to Lou's well-meaning proposal (Why not marry Maria? You still love her, after all?) with unspeakable vulgarity. This was Hugo at his worst, one more *ressentiment*. He was offended and lost all semblance of civilized behavior. Fischer and his new wife would have been scandalized and uncomprehending. What sort of fuss was Comrade Huppert making, in a situation that was perfectly ordinary?

Ordinary, certainly, in their own circle and in the wider diaspora of exiled Communist intellectuals. For years, men like Fischer or Frei had been living under false identities, hardly ever using their real names, and moving in and out with various female companions, marrying right and left. Fischer and Frei were not pistol-carrying secret agents, but many of their friends were, including Fischer's first wife, Ruth, who had been sent into Nazi Germany on spying missions. Accustomed to danger, deception, and secrecy, such people only took up with each other and seemed to have left behind the norms of peacetime behavior.

While Hugo Huppert never lived under a false identity, never acted as a secret agent of the Comintern, he could hardly claim to have lived a bourgeois life in exile, except, perhaps, during the years of his marriage to Vera. Just exactly why he rebelled against the suggestion of resuming his liaison with Maria is not entirely clear. He himself probably could not have said why he became abusive that day in the spring of 1956. Perhaps things would have turned out differently if Ernst Fischer had not been involved, but Hugo's painful rejection of the woman he had dreamed about for seven years may be understood as part of a sweeping rejection of most other wartime contingencies.

He was a free man at last. He had left fear behind. A very long chapter of his life had ended. He was back in Vienna, this time for good. Instead of resuming his passionate affair with Maria, he would turn, soon enough, to another woman, Josephine Plachy, who was the mother of a fifteen-year-old boy. He married Josephine ("Finny") and settled down for good, a very surprising turn of events after an interminable succession of young lovers in the Soviet Union. His decision to marry and set up housekeeping with Finny and her son seems a rejection of his lifelong behavior. He was suddenly changing course.

As far as he was concerned, his life in wartime and exile had now come to an end. Twenty years later, when he was writing his autobiography, he would close the three-volume narrative precisely on that day in April 1956 when he rejected Maria. This was his homecoming. He was resigning from a life of fear and passion. He would remain a Communist, but he would settle down into a quiet, one might say bourgeois, existence in his new Viennese home.

I think I understand his decision to close the books on the story of his life in midstream. He never conceived of his autobiographical memoir as simply his story. He meant it as a record of all the terrible events his generation experienced, told through his own peregrinations, his own losses, his own fears. Now that Hitler and Stalin were dead and gone, now that peace had returned for the survivors, he could return to normalcy, to a private life without interest to his readers.

Does this mean that the last twenty years of his life were of little consequence? Far from it. Those were the years when he published copiously. His translation and adaptation of the Georgian national epic had already come out in Berlin. His translations and adaptations of Russian poetry, especially of Mayakovsky's works, also brought out by publishing houses in East Germany, rolled off the presses regularly. His own poetry followed, book after book. Throughout, he wrote for the weekly *Weltbühne*, whose editor, Hans Leonard, appreciated the poet's journalism, especially the clever way in which he managed to embrace the Party line, quietly, unobtrusively.

A fine example of this is his article in *Die Weltbühne* of December 19, 1956. Under the title of *Flüchtlinge*—"refugees"—he describes his encounters with the men, women, and children fleeing the Soviet tanks that were crushing the Hungarian uprising of that fateful year. His assignment, it would seem, was to find ways of deflecting the international outcry caused by the brutal Soviet intervention. Here, then, is his take on the events in Hungary.

He begins by setting the mood. It is a cloudy day, he writes. The fields on the Austrian side of the border are snow-covered. Under the snow there may be land mines. This stretch of borderlands, full of marshes, has rarely been under surveillance on the Austrian side. The silent migration of fleeing Hungarians across the border is witnessed only by migratory birds up above. The Austrian border guards hardly react to the stream of fleeing Hungarian families. The guards are exhausted, tired of stopping the Hungarians to ask for passports and visas; they have given up trying to understand the papers. No one knows exactly where these people are coming from or where they are headed. Later, in the afternoon, back in the city, the reporter follows a group of refugees. They stand silently in front of the lighted Christmas shop windows. This is a foreign setting for them. They enter a café. Hugo follows, accompanied by a Hungarian-speaking assistant. He invites two of the Hungarian men, father and son, to join him and his assistant.

Having established the reporter's credibility, he turns to the job at hand, which is to find a way to deflect the impact of the brutal Soviet assault for his readers in Berlin. And so he writes about well-dressed Hungarian families who can be heard and seen now in the better Viennese hotels, and who can also be found in the banks and in the waiting rooms of Western consulates. They, too, describe themselves as refugees. They leave behind, he claims, illegal commercial deals and they have taken care to put their foreign currencies and their jewelry in safe boxes in West Germany and Switzerland. Such people should by rights appear before the authorities. But they will be gone in the morning. They had crossed the border in their private cars, with proper papers and twelve suitcases, to be sure.

Some of the well-dressed refugees are not so lucky. They do not look forward to wealth in the West. They are bitter and thoroughly disappointed. Whose fault? They accuse the West and its politicians who promised help as the Soviet tanks showed up in the streets of Budapest. Radio Free Europe had given the impression that help was on the way. Such people no doubt had counted on a small World War III to reinstate them into the possession of their estates and factories, writes Hugo, with a heavy dose of sarcasm.

There is no need to say more. The poet Hugo Huppert follows the Party line. At this point in the Cold War, when the world was watching to see whether Stalin's successors would continue to depend on tanks and guns, the answer was clear. Countering the fallout from the Soviet invasion of Hungary was certainly a demanding task. In later years, Hugo would find it much easier to insert the Party line into innocuous-seeming articles written for the weekly *Weltbühne*, especially as his reports from Italy, sponsored by *Die Weltbühne*, acquired a large following in Communist East Germany. Brought out eventually as a book, those reports from sunny Italy would have been much appreciated in Communist East Germany, just as the Berlin Wall arose to stand between its citizens and the outside world.

As for our author, he had found a perfectly viable solution to living a normal life, after half a century of danger and deprivation. He remained in the Party, which continued to be his home, as comfortable as a snail's transportable carapace, but he lived in free Vienna and traveled frequently, in Italy, mostly, but also to Paris, Prague, and Moscow. His income came from Communist publishing houses. And yet he remained a free man: he did not have to deal with the Communist politicians, not with Fischer, nor with Becher or Kurella. He no longer lived danger-ously. And he could devote himself entirely to the pleasures of writing, no longer for his notebooks, but for volume after volume coming out in Leipzig and Berlin.

Did he have regrets? Did he feel exposed to the contempt of contem-poraries, of colleagues and friends who had, at last, chosen to break with Stalin's successors? Especially after the Hungarian and Polish attempts to break free, especially after the Prague Spring brought to a halt by Soviet tanks? No, Comrade Huppert remained steadfast, right up to the end. His private thoughts he kept to himself. As he put it, citing the Swiss writer Max Frisch: "This is an honest book, reader: and what does it hide and why?"

Only very rarely does Hugo face a crushing condemnation of his political choices. Not in the press, not in public, but, in one unforget-table instance, noted in his diary: it was in Paris, where he was visit-ing the poet Paul Celan. After a fairly contentious discussion of poetic techniques, Hugo turned to the man many consider the greatest poet of our time in the German language and asked him to sign one of his books with a dedication for Hugo. Celan refused. He considered Hugo a Stalinist. True enough? Or too simple a dismissal of a lifetime of choices made under extreme conditions?

REFERENCES

ARCHIVAL SOURCES

Hugo Huppert Archiv, Akademie der Künste, Berlin

This is a large archival collection that includes diaries from as far back as the 1920s and many letters to and from Huppert. The only period of Huppert's life that is poorly documented in this collection is his seven-year exile in Soviet Georgia. Among the files I found particularly useful are the following:

File # 22 (photos, undated)
File # 64 (diary entries, Moscow, 1933)
File # 98 (letters from his father, 1928)
File # 110 (letters to his brother Josef, 1941)
File # 115 (diary entries, Paris, 1927)
File # 144 (letters from Finny, Vienna, 1961)
File # 183 (diary entries, Moscow, 1940)
File # 191 (diary entries, 1931)
File # 196 (diary entries, Moscow, 1937)
File # 209 (diary entries on the eve of Emily's departure for Moscow, Christmas 1927, and on Hugo's nervous breakdown, at home in Bielitz, New Year's Eve 1927, January 1928)
File # 210 (diary entries on Hugo's arrival in Paris and his despair, November 1925–April 1926)
File # 211 (diary entries after Emily's death, Moscow, 1929)
File # 212 (diary entries regarding various seductions, Moscow, 1932)
File # 220 (diary entries regarding Vera, Moscow, 1930)
File # 221 (diary entries, Moscow, 1930s, winter with coal miners)
File # 222 (diary entries, membership in Soviet Communist Party, 1930)
File # 223 (diary entries, trouble with Vera, colleagues, 1930s)
File # 231 (letters from Adolf Huppert, pointing out Hugo's failings, 1920s)

File # 232 (photos, undated)
File # 246 (letters to Emily, Vienna, 1922)
File # 248 (letters to Emily, 1923)
File # 252 (diary entries, Salzburg, summer 1923; transcript of interview, West German radio, 1973)
File # 277 (diary entries, Lwów, undated)
File # 289 (diary entries, Moscow, 1938)
File # 305 (letters from the 1920s)
File # 306 (letter from Maxie, 1926)
File # 346 (letters to Bredel, Vienna, 1956)
File # 348 (correspondence with Arnold Zweig, 1959)
File # 362 (correspondence with Paul Celan, 1966)
File # 365 (letter to Otto Schneid, letter from Margit Reich, Vienna, April 1966)

PUBLISHED SOURCES

Works by Hugo Huppert

Hugo Huppert's memoirs, consisting of three tightly packed volumes, *Die Angelehnte Tür* (1976), *Wanduhr Mit Vordergrund* (1977), and *Schach Dem Doppelgänger* (1979), stand out among Hugo's published works. They speak to the reader very directly. One can sense the passion poured into those pages. They are Hugo's best works—not surprising, really, since he is at last writing about his favorite subject.

Without claiming completeness, here is a list of his published works, including the three-volume memoirs, each volume of which is listed as a separate title. The titles are listed chronologically by original publication date.

Sibirische Mannschaft: ein Skizzenbuch aus dem Kusbass. Moscow and Leningrad: Verlagsgenossenschaft Ausländischer Arbeiter, 1934.
Jahreszeiten: Gedichte. Moscow: Verl Das Internationale Buch, 1941.
Georgischer Wanderstab: Ein Buch west-östlicher Zeitgedichte. Berlin: Volk und Welt, 1954.
Schota Rusthaweli: Der Recke im Tigerfell. Berlin: Verlag Rütten & Loening, 1955.
Kerngesundes Land: Ein Oesterreicher grüsst die DDR. Halle and Leipzig: Mitteldeutscher Verlag, 1961.
Münzen im Brunnen: Erlebtes Italien. Berlin: Aufbau Verlag, 1962/63.
Wladimir Majakowski in Selbstzeugnissen und Bilddokumenten. Reinbek bei Hamburg: Rowohlt, 1965.
Wladimir Majakowski: Poeme und Gedichte. 5 vols. Berlin: Verlag Volk und Welt, 1966–1973.
Logarithmus der Freude: Gedichte. Berlin: Verlag Volk und Welt, 1968.
Wladimir Majakowskij: Poet und Tribun. Berlin: Aufbau-Verlag, 1968.
Andre Bewandtnis: Lyrik. Halle and Leipzig: Mitteldeutscher Verlag, 1970.
Rhapsodie: Brot und Rosen. Poem. Berlin: Verlag Rütten & Loening, 1972.

Sinnen und Trachten: Anmerkungen zur Poetologie. Halle and Leipzig: Mitteldeutscher Verlag, 1973.

Wolkenbahn und Erdenstrasse: Gedichte und Poeme. Halle and Leipzig: Mitteldeutscher Verlag, 1975.

Bannmeile und Horizont: Ausgewählte Prosa. Halle and Leipzig: Mitteldeutscher
Verlag, 1976.

Die Angelehnte Tür: Bericht von einer Jugend. Halle and Leipzig: Mitteldeutscher
Verlag, 1976.

Ungeduld des Jahrhunderts: Erinnerungen an Majakowski. Berlin: Henschel Verlag,
1976.

Wanduhr Mit Vordergrund: Stationen eines Lebens. Halle: Mitteldeutscher Verlag,
1977.

Minuten und Momente: Ausgewählte Publizistik. Halle and Leipzig: Mitteldeutscher
Verlag, 1978.

Schach Dem Doppelgänger: Anläufe der Reifezeit. Halle and Leipzig, Mitteldeutscher
Verlag, 1979.

Indizien oder Vollmond auf Bestellung: Gedichte. Halle and Leipzig: Mitteldeutscher
Verlag, 1981.

"Wien örtlich": Gedichte und lyrische Texte. Eisenstadt: Edition Roetzer, 1981.

Works by Contemporaries

Borkenau, Franz. *The Spanish Cockpit*. London: Faber and Faber, 1937. Borkenau
was a student of Grünberg's in Vienna and an official of the Comintern before he
broke with the Communists in 1929 and moved to Paris with his wife, Lucie. Both
husband and wife were historians. Borkenau went off to Spain and reported on
the Spanish Civil War.

Ehrenburg, Ilya. *Memoirs, 1921–1941*. Cleveland: World Publishing Company, 1964.

Fischer, Ernst. *Das Ende einer Illusion: Erinnerungen 1945–1955*. Vienna, Munich,
and Zurich: Molden, 1973. Fischer, married to Ruth von Mayenburg at the time,
shared Hugo's Moscow exile and returned to Vienna at war's end to assume political office. In this, his last book, he gives up on Communism.

Freud, Sigmund, and Arnold Zweig. *Briefwechsel [von Sigmund Freud und Arnold
Zweig]*. Ed. Ernst L. Freud. Frankfurt: Fischer, 1968.

Herdan-Zuckmayer, Alice. *Genies sind im Lehrplan nicht vorgesehen*. Frankfurt:
Fischer, 1979. She began as a student at the Schwarzwald School at the age of eight
and later became a successful actress. Married to the playwright Carl Zuckmayer,
she looked back, in her later years, at her life in Vienna and to the powerful guidance provided by Frau Doktor Schwarzwald. Her memoir is an absolute delight.

Kisch, Egon Erwin. *Abenteuer in fünf Kontinenten, Reportagen*. Vienna: Globus Verlag, 1948. A brief sample of Kisch's writings, edited and with an introduction by
Hugo Huppert.

Koestler, Arthur. *Arrow in the Blue: An Autobiography*. New York: Random House,
1952.

Schnitzler, Arthur. *Der Weg ins Freie*. Berlin: S. Fischer, 1922.

———. *Tagebuch*. Vol. 8. Vienna: Oesterreichische Akademie der Wissenschaften, 1981.

Von Mayenburg, Ruth. *Blaues Blut und Rote Fahnen: Ein Leben unter vielen namen. Mit 44 Dokumentarbildern*. Vienna: Molden, 1969. The remarkable memoir of an aristocrat with nerves of steel who knew Hugo Huppert in Moscow and described him as the most anxious human being she had ever known.

Zweig, Arnold. *Caliban, oder, Politik und Leidenschaft: Versuch über die menschlichen Gruppenleidenschaften dargetan am Antisemitismus*. Potsdam: G. Kiepenheuer, 1927.

Secondary Works

Bronsen, David. *Joseph Roth: Eine Biographie*. Cologne: Kiepenheuer und Witsch, 1974.

Červinka, František. "The Hilsner Affair." *Leo Baeck Yearbook* 13 (1968): 142–157.

Chalfen, Israel. *Paul Celan: Eine Biographie seiner Jugend*. Frankfurt am Main: Insel Verlag, 1979.

Frei, Bruno. *Der Papiersäbel: Autobiographie*. Frankfurt am Main: S. Fischer, 1972.

Friedman, Philip. *Die galizischen Juden im Kampfe um ihre Gleichberechtigung (1848–1868)*. Frankfurt: J. Kaufman Verlag, 1929.

Handler, Andrew. *Blood Libel in Tiszaeszlar*. New York: Columbia University Press, 1980.

Hartewig, Karin. *Zurückgekehrt: Die Geschichte der Jüdischen Kommunisten in der DDR*. Cologne: Böhlau, 2000.

Holmes, Deborah. *Langeweile ist Gift: Das Leben der Eugenie Schwarzwald*. St. Pölten: Residenz Verlag, 2012. This biography of a remarkable woman, "Frau Doktor" Schwarzwald, is a translation of the original English monograph. Dr. Schwarzwald founded a school for gifted girls before the First World War in Vienna. The composer Arnold Schönberg, the painter Oskar Kokoschka, and the architect Adolf Loos were on the faculty. Professor Kelsen was closely involved with Schwarzwald's enterprise. Both he and Hugo visited Dr. Schwarzwald's summer artists' colony in the mountains, as did, among others, Rudolf Serkin, the musical prodigy whose later career in America is well known and who as a boy was the darling of the Schwarzwald School.

Holzner, Johann, "Geglückte integration in der UdSSR-gestörte Integration in Österreich. Anmerkungen zu Hugo Huppert." In *Leben im Exil: Probleme der Integration deutscher Flüchtlinge im Ausland, 1933–1945*, edited by Wolfgang Frühwald and Wolfgang Schieder, 122–130. Hamburg: Hoffmann und Campe, 1981. This article concerns Hugo Huppert's remarkably successful assimilation in Russia.

Jarmatz, Klaus, Simone Barck, and Peter Diezel, eds. *Exil in der UdSSR*. Frankfurt am Main: Röderburg, 1979. This comprehensive account of the work of German and Austrian Communist writers in Soviet exile was put together, laboriously, by a large team, from a Communist viewpoint.

Korzec, Pawel. *Juifs en Pologne: La question juive pendant l'entre-deux-guerres*. Paris: Presses de la Fondation Nationale des Sciences Politiques, 1980.

Krüll, Marianne. *Freud and His Father*. New York: W. W. Norton, 1986.

Kuhn, Walter. *Geschichte der Deutschen Sprachinsel Bielitz (Schlesien)*. Würzburg: Holzner, 1981. I have relied on this study for a detailed account of life in Bielitz.

Kurth, Peter. *American Cassandra: The Life of Dorothy Thompson*. Boston: Little, Brown, 1990. This astonishingly detailed biography brings to life the wild lives of the great journalist and of her husband, Sinclair Lewis, as well as those of her many friends, especially those in Vienna, including, above all, Genia Schwarzwald.

La Grange, Henry-Louis de. *Gustav Mahler: Chronique d'une vie. I, 1860–1900*. Paris: Fayard 1979. Note page 13, the author's misdating of the Polná murder of 1900: "Un juif fut encore accusé au 18e siècle du meurtre rituel d'un enfant chrétien."

Marcus, Joseph. *Social and Political History of the Jews in Poland, 1919–1939*. New York: Mouton, 1983.

Masaryk, T. G. *Die Bedeutung des Polnaer Verbrechens für den Ritualaberglauben*. Berlin: H. S. Hermann, 1900.

Nussbaum, Arthur. *Der Polnaer Ritualmordprozess: Eine kriminalpsychologische Untersuchung auf aktenmässiger Grundlage*. Berlin: A. W. Hayn's Erben, 1906.

Oxaal, Ivar, Michael Pollak, and Gerhard Botz, eds. *Jews, Antisemitism and Culture in Vienna*. London: Routledge & Kegan Paul, 1987.

Parker, Stephen. *Bertolt Brecht: A Literary Life*. London: Bloomsbury, 2014.

Pike, David. *German Writers in Soviet Exile, 1933–1945*. Chapel Hill: University of North Carolina Press, 1982.

———. *The Politics of Culture in Soviet-Occupied Germany, 1945–1949*. Stanford, Calif.: Stanford University Press, 1982. Especially useful on the political career of Johannes R. Becher, who was Hugo's boss in Moscow.

Schlögel, Karl. *Moscow 1937*. Cambridge: Polity, 2012.

Schöttler, Peter. *Lucie Varga: Les autorités invisibles*. Paris: Editions du Cerf, 1991. This remarkable study reveals the short life of an exceptional intellectual: a graduate of the Schwarzwald School and the University of Vienna, she came to Paris with Franz Borkenau and worked with Lucien Febvre, publishing articles in his journal, the *Annales*, before fleeing to Toulouse as the Nazis arrived in Paris.

Snyder, Timothy. *Bloodlands: Europe between Hitler and Stalin*. New York: Basic Books, 2010. Thoroughly convincing account of the decimation of millions who fell victim to Hitler and Stalin.

Wagner, Renate. *Arthur Schnitzler: Eine Biographie*. Vienna: Molden, 1981.

Weigel, Hans. *Karl Kraus, oder, Die Machte der Ohnmacht: Versuch eines Motivenberichts zur Erhellung eines vielfachen Lebenswerks*. Vienna: Molden, 1968.

Wistrich, Robert. *Socialism and the Jews: The Dilemmas of Assimilation in Germany and Austria-Hungary*. Rutherford, N.J.: Fairleigh Dickinson University Press, 1982.

INDEX

German Communist Party, 4, 71, 138
German-Soviet non-aggression pact of
1939, 5, 101–103
Glaubauf, Hans, 75
Gloffner, Nathan, 61
Gramsci, Antonio, 68
Great Depression, 4, 95
Gregorig (Czech deputy), 50
Gromov, Ivan, 95
Grünberg, Karl, 70–71, 110

Haar, Karl, 60
Hapsburg Empire. See Austrian Empire
Heine, Heinrich, 19–20
Herzl, Theodor, 62–63
Hilsner, Leopold, 43–46
Hirschfeld, Rabbi, 84
Hitler, Adolf, 2, 4, 50, 68, 140; Austrian
takeover of, 5, 100; seizure of power
by, 89, 92, 95. See also World War II
The House of the Dead (Dostoyevsky), 98
Hrachovsky, Father, 39–40
Hruza, Agnes, 43–45
Huberman, Bronislaw, 75
Huberman, Stanislaw, 75
Hugo Huppert Archive, Berlin, 3, 53–55
L'Humanité, 4, 78–79
Hungarian Uprising of 1956, 141–42
Huppert, Abraham/Adolf, 9–31, 74, 84,
102–104; antisemitism and, 41; assimi-
lation in Bielitz of, 19–21; civil service
job of, 19, 23, 56, 64; correspondence
with HH of, 88–89; expatriation and
name change of, 13–19; military ser-
vice of, 15–19, 29
Huppert, Anna, 14–31, 74, 84, 102; death
of, 104; in HH's memoirs, 56–58
Huppert, Annette, 92, 106, 109–10, 119,
121, 128
Huppert, Emily. See Artbauer, Emily
Huppert, Emmanuel, 10–11, 14, 20, 58,
77, 118
Huppert, Hugo, 1–6; archive in Berlin of,
3, 53–55; assimilated family of, 9–31;

autobiography of, 1–2, 6, 17n, 135, 137,
140; Bielitz childhood, 1–2, 53–65; education and intellectual development
of, 57–63; German education of, 24;
music and, 57–58, 69; politicization
of, 3–5, 64–65; Soviet citizenship of,
5, 136; student life in Paris of, 76–79;
student life in Vienna of, 3, 64–65,
69–76; well-traveled suitcase of, 65.
See also diaries of HH; personal qualities of HH; writing of HH
Huppert, Jacob, 10, 21, 41
Huppert, Josef, 5, 75, 101–107, 118
Huppert, Leopold, 25
Huppert, Lilian, 5, 101–102, 104–106
Huppert, Paula, 58, 77, 118
Hušek (Czech antisemite), 44

Institute of Red Professors, 92–94
International Anti-Jewish
Congress, 38
Internationale Literatur/Deutsche Blätter,
89, 99
islands of memory, 54
Izviestia, 95, 99

Janda, Karl, 43–44
Jaurès, Jean, 78, 88

Kant, Immanuel, 19–20
Kelsen, Hans, 68, 70–71, 75, 81, 110
Kisch, Egon Erwin, 63, 70, 96, 132–33
Klofač (editor of Narodny Listy), 40
The Knight in the Tiger Skin (Vitiaz' v
tigrovoi shkure) (Rustaveli), 2, 6,
129–36, 141
Koestler, Arthur, 5
Kokoschka, Oskar, 81
Konjev, Ivan, 118
Koplenig, Johann, 117
Körber, Isi, 60–61
Körber, Lilli, 60–61
Körner, Theodor, 119
Kosciuszko, Tadeusz, 15

GEORGE HUPPERT is Professor of History Emeritus at the University of Illinois at Chicago and author of several books, including *The Idea of Perfect History: Historical Erudition and Historical Philosophy in Renaissance France* (1970), *The Style of Paris: Renaissance Origins of the French Enlightenment* (1999), *Public Schools in Renaissance France* (1984), *After the Black Death: A Social History of Early Modern Europe* (1986), and *Les Bourgeois Gentilshommes: An Essay on the Definition of Elites in Renaissance France* (1977). He has published many articles in scholarly journals and has served as the president of the Historical Society and as the editor of its journal. He has been a Guggenheim, Woodrow Wilson, NEH, and ACLS Fellow, and served as a visiting professor at the Collège de France, in Paris.